PRAISE

PERFORMANCE T

'A very useful introduction that brings the subject to life for those less experienced in the area or looking to establish a performance management framework in their organization, as well as being useful for those working in companies with established performance management processes to ensure that these deliver as expected (particularly through the oh-so-crucial alignment between performance management and organizational goals).' **Daniela Freudenthaler, Corporate HR Europe, Manager Strategy and Targets, BMW Group**

'This book has expertly threaded all the elements of performance management together in a practical and interactive way by using activities, diagnostics, case studies and scenarios to encourage HR professionals and line managers to embed great performance practices.' **Esther O'Halloran, Director, EOH Business Solutions, former Managing Director, PAUL Bakery**

'*Performance Management* is packed with information that delivers immediate benefits to both practising professionals and human resource management students. This well-structured and comprehensive traverse of the landscape of performance management in organizations with practical examples and compelling case studies is a must-read for all professionals dealing with people on a day-to-day basis.' **Dr Chandana Sanyal, Senior Lecturer in Human Resource Management and Development, Middlesex University Business School**

'People are (and will always be, even in this age of technology) an organization's most valuable asset. Linda Ashdown's excellent book is your practical guide to nurturing your talented people and driving organizational effectiveness. I thoroughly recommend that this book sits on your desk, with scribbles, notes and folded corners for daily use!' **Simon Francis, Chief Executive Officer, Flock Associates Ltd**

'This book is full of practical information about performance management with some excellent case studies. A very important and timely contribution to this area.' **Ramya S Yarlagadda, Head of HR and Strategy, International School of Hyderabad**

Second Edition

PERFORMANCE MANAGEMENT

A practical introduction

Linda Ashdown

Publisher's note

Every possible effort has been made to ensure that the information contained in this book is accurate at the time of going to press, and the publisher and authors cannot accept responsibility for any errors or omissions, however caused. No responsibility for loss or damage occasioned to any person acting, or refraining from action, as a result of the material in this publication can be accepted by the editor, the publisher or any of the authors.

First published in Great Britain and the United States in 2014 by Kogan Page Limited
Second edition published in 2018

2nd Floor, 45 Gee Street
London EC1V 3RS
United Kingdom
www.koganpage.com

c/o Martin P Hill Consulting
122 W 27th St, 10th Floor
New York NY 10001
USA

4737/23 Ansari Road
Daryaganj
New Delhi 110002
India

© Linda Ashdown, 2014, 2018

The right of Linda Ashdown to be identified as the author of this work has been asserted by her in accordance with the Copyright, Designs and Patents Act 1988.

ISBN   978 0 7494 8337 1
E-ISBN   978 0 7494 8338 8

British Library Cataloguing-in-Publication Data

A CIP record for this book is available from the British Library.

Library of Congress Cataloging-in-Publication Data
Names: Ashdown, Linda, author.
Title: Performance management : a practical introduction / Linda Ashdown.
Description: Second edition. | London ; New York : Kogan Page, 2018. |
   Includes bibliographical references and index.
Identifiers: LCCN 2018019055 (print) | LCCN 2018020932 (ebook) | ISBN
   9780749483388 (ebook) | ISBN 9780749483371 (pbk.)
Subjects: LCSH: Performance–Management. | Employees–Rating of. | Personnel
   management.
Classification: LCC HF5549.5.P35 (ebook) | LCC HF5549.5.P35 A84 2018 (print)
   | DDC 658.3–dc23

Typeset by Integra Software Services, Pondicherry
Print production managed by Jellyfish
Printed and bound by CPI Group (UK) Ltd, Croydon, CR0 4YY

CONTENTS

*Downloadable resources are available at **www.koganpage.com/ PerformanceManagement***

ACKNOWLEDGEMENTS

I am so grateful to the people who gave me their time and support through new case studies, interviews and thought pieces during the writing of this updated edition of *Performance Management*. Thank you to Professor Sir Cary Cooper, Anila DeHart and Andrew Erhardt-Lewis at Deloitte, David Morison and Gurjit Sandhu at Jumeirah, Charlotte Martin FCIPD, Brad Taylor and Edward Houghton from CIPD and Rebecca Grigg at Hilton. Thank you also to the amazing bunch of fun, talented people I work with at CIPD.

Love and thanks always, to Mark, Catherine and David for always being there supporting me.

What is performance management?

Since I wrote the first edition of this book four years ago, much has changed in the world. There is a new president in the White House, the UK voted to 'Brexit' and the threat of acts of terror feels all too prevalent in our lives, wherever we live in the world. The world of work has also changed significantly in that short space of time and looks likely to continue to rapidly change as we move further into the 21st century.

> We are living through a fundamental transformation in the way we work. Automation and 'thinking machines' are replacing human tasks and jobs, and changing the skills that organizations are looking for in their people. These momentous changes raise huge organizational, talent and HR challenges – at a time when business leaders are already wrestling with unprecedented risks, disruption and political and societal upheaval.
>
> (PWC, 2017)

As I write, there is growing debate over the nature of employment relationships, particularly in light of the growth in the gig economy. More women than ever are returning to work after childbirth. Technology continues to transform how work is carried out. Expectations of new generations of workers are impacting significantly on workplaces and multi-generational workforces present new challenges. For my parents' generation, working for one employer all their working lives was not unusual; for my children they will not only be likely to have many different employers during their working lives, they may well change careers several times, and could well hold several different jobs at the same time. Attending a GCSE presentation evening at my son's school, the Headmaster spoke of the challenge of education systems needing to prepare students for jobs that currently don't exist. Against this backdrop of change, however, there is a constant. I firmly believe that the effective management of performance at an organization, team and individual level, both now and in the future, will be vital not only for organization success but also survival.

This book has been updated to reflect current thinking and approaches to performance management. There has been much debate around the use of the performance appraisal for example, and whilst some have reported on its demise, it still forms a key element of many organizations' approach to performance management. There is also a much greater focus on ethics in this edition to reflect how this has risen in importance for organizations, their employees and customers in recent years. It is also at the heart of the CIPD 'Profession for the Future' work : 'ethical cultures are vital in helping businesses shift focus from short-term profits to long-term sustainability' (CIPD, 2017a). There are new case studies, interviews, thought pieces and activities to support the reader in enabling effective performance management in their workplaces.

This book breaks down performance management into some core aspects and explores practically how performance management can be best used to deliver positive organizational outcomes. Having worked as an HR director, as a lecturer/tutor and more recently for the CIPD, I understand the value and importance of research. However, it is also so important that the research is used appropriately and effectively in the world of work. Evidence-based HR practices can and should enable us to better manage people in organizations and encourage the performance that organizations require to reach their goals and fulfil their missions.

Whilst there is reference to contemporary research and further reading in this book, it is not intended to provide an academic focus for performance management. Rather, it is intended to equip you the reader with a sound practical grasp of the practice of managing performance in organizations today. I offer my personal viewpoints but have aimed to provide you with a balance of views, options and approaches, as there is no one-size-fits-all solution here. This book breaks down performance management into some core aspects and explores how performance management can be best used to deliver positive organizational outcomes. Within the chapters are a variety of examples and activities such as diagnostic questionnaires, reflection and action planning to enable you to take the learning and apply it to your work experiences.

This first chapter aims to explore the concept of performance management in general terms. To begin our journey we need to first identify what is meant by the term. This is not necessarily a straightforward task, as performance management covers a wide range of activities and its exact nature will often vary between organizations.

Defining performance management

Performance management is made up of many activities that when managed holistically can lead to effective people management. The particular challenge of providing a clear, comprehensive definition of performance management is that it covers such a breadth of activities. It is also difficult to define precisely as the nature of performance management will and should vary according to the organization context. The sector, structure, size, culture, strategy and leadership of the organization will all influence the nature of performance management. One of the most often used definitions is that of Armstrong (2009): 'Performance Management is a systematic process for improving organizational performance by developing the performance of individuals and teams.' One of the reasons this definition has proved so popular is because at its heart is the crucial issue of the link between the performance of an organization's human resources and the achievement of organization goals. 'Alignment' is a key ingredient in successful performance management systems: the alignment of an individual's performance to the goals of the organization.

A senior director I worked with in the advertising industry once told me that he regarded effective performance management as having an invisible thread linking the organization's mission statement to the performance objectives of the individual – and that image has stayed with me both in my practice as an HR professional and when teaching human resource management (HRM) to others. I firmly believe that the core principle of everyone working for an organization having a clear understanding of how they contribute to the mission, vision and goals of the organization is an important one. There is a real benefit to the organization of having all the people who work for it focused on the right things to add value. There are also clear benefits for the employees of that invisible thread being in place. For example, the intrinsic satisfaction of feeling significant, understanding their contribution and ultimately feeling valued by the organization – that invisible thread helps to deliver that understanding and those feelings. This is a powerful enabler for retaining staff and supporting them to deliver high-performance outcomes. Individuals are much more likely to 'go the extra mile' for those organizations where they understand and value the organization's goals and believe that they can contribute to the achievement of those goals and will be valued for doing so. Unfortunately, in many organizations that connection between the organization's goals and individual contribution is either weak or missing altogether; this has the potential to impact detrimentally on both the performance of the individual and that of the organization.

A good starting point for a definition of performance management might be to consider what is meant by the term 'performance'. Historically the emphasis has been very much on output or results. Management by objectives was very popular in the 1970s, but fell out of favour during the 1990s as it drifted into over-bureaucratization and focused on the quantifiable whilst neglecting the more qualitative elements of performance. Whilst achievement of objectives and outputs remains a key deliverable for performance management, organizations today are also increasingly concerned with the 'inputs', the behaviours, 'how people carry out their jobs'. This is reflected in Brumbach's (1998: 265) definition of performance: 'performance means both behaviours and results... Not just the instruments for results, behaviours are also outcomes in their own right.' In an economy where knowledge and service are key, competitive advantage comes not only through results, but through the behaviours people demonstrate when carrying out their roles. If we are to encourage effective performance in our workplaces we need to focus not only on what people do, but how they do it (the role of competencies will be explored in more detail in Chapter 6).

The historical context

To understand performance management today it is helpful to consider the historical backdrop of approaches to management and organization behaviour. Arguably, the first real sense we get of a formalization of the management of performance comes with F W Taylor (1856–1917) and the scientific school of management. Taylor believed that effective performance would come from a very structured approach to the design of work, with workers having very specific tasks to complete, with specific targets to reach and clearly identified financial reward. Motivation was driven by a simple economic transaction with workers carrying out their roles in the most effective way possible to reach the highest possible wages. Whilst we recognize that managing performance is an activity of much greater complexity today, it is important not to lose sight of the fact that there are many working relationships that are reliant on the delivery of a basic transaction for effective performance.

The Human Relations School led to a much greater focus on social factors at work and on the behaviour of employees within an organization. Rather than just focusing on the rational, the complexity of humans – their psychological and social needs – were recognized as important factors in organization performance. The famous Hawthorne Experiments conducted in the late 1920s at the Western Electric Company, near Chicago, highlighted the importance of human relationships in the workplace. In one experiment, referred to as the bank-wiring observation room, a group of men were offered a financial incentive to earn more money based on greater productivity. In the world of Taylor we would have expected to see a rise in performance levels as a result of this incentive; however, this did not happen. Group pressure was exerted to ensure performance levels were not increased. The power of so-called 'group norms' was exerted. These experiments generated new ideas relating to managing performance, particularly the importance of informal work groups, but also the vital role of managers in motivation and performance management.

Despite the impact of the Human Relations School, most early formal performance monitoring systems evolved from Taylorism. In the 1800s there were stick systems in some factories, where at the end of the day the supervisor would place a coloured stick by the work bench of the worker to indicate how they had performed during that session; for example, blue for good, yellow for satisfactory and black for poor, indicating that your services might not be called for the next shift! I am hoping things have moved on a little since then! Merit rating was popular in the United States and the UK in the 1950s and 1960s and involved an assessment of performance based on a tick-box rating scheme against particular qualities or traits. There is a strong sense here of a 'school report' approach, the individual being judged by a superior. Whilst the trend has been away from such an approach in recent times, Armstrong (2009) argues that some of the competency rating schemes used today 'look suspiciously like some of the traits identified 70 years or more ago'.

Management by objectives (MBO) is an important stage in the development of performance management. It is a system or style of management that attempts to relate the goals of an organization to the performance of an individual. The following elements form a key part of the MBO process:

- setting of clear objectives and targets;
- the active participation of both individual and managers in the formation and agreement of these targets;
- the regular monitoring and review of performance against targets set;
- a backdrop of meaningful reward to support the process.

Much of today's performance management process can be seen here in MBO. The requirement for clear objectives, agreement and regular review are still a vital part of performance management today. However, after being incredibly popular in the 1960s and 1970s, MBO gradually fell out of favour. The significant factors in the demise of MBO appear to have been the pure focus on the measurable and quantifiable at the expense of the more qualitative aspects of performance, an emphasis on output without consideration of input. Many systems drowned in bureaucracy, with form-filling becoming an end in itself, and a resultant lack of valuable output from the process. MBO in many cases became a top-down form of assessment with little contribution from the individual or consideration of his or her individual needs and aspirations. MBO was targeted mostly at line managers, so other roles within the organization were often not included in a structured performance management system. This was not a performance management process for all employees.

It wasn't until the latter half of the 1980s that performance management as we understand it today became a recognized process. In 1992 the Institute of Personnel Management (IPM) produced the following definition of Performance Management: 'A strategy which relates to every activity of the organization set in the context of its human resources policies, culture, style and communication systems. The nature of the strategy depends on the organizational context and can vary from organization to organization.'

The research conducted by the IPM in 1992 identified that typical performance management processes would include individual objective setting linked to the wider goals of the organization, performance reviews and integration with training, development and reward outcomes. Performance management was becoming a much more holistic activity, incorporated a range of HRM activity and was targeted at all employees rather than just managers. Over the last 20 years there has also been a gradual shift away from a judgemental approach to a problem-solving approach with both manager and the individual being active participants in reviewing performance and setting objectives. Direction and feedback remain important processes; however, it is now largely recognized that the individual should be an active participant providing input into the performance management process. Consensus and co-operation have increasingly replaced the concept of control in performance management.

In more recent times three key themes have emerged in the development and enactment of performance management in organizations: 1) the importance of aligning performance activity to strategic goals (explored in greater depth in Chapter 3 when we look at the 'fit' between performance management and organization strategy); 2) the vital role of line managers in implementing performance management and the importance of trust in the relationship between employee and line manager (considered later in this chapter when we look at who is involved with the performance management process); 3) there has been a significant shift away from the concept of a heavy reliance and focus on an annual appraisal towards a drive for ongoing performance discussions between managers and employees. A hunger for regular feedback and agile goal setting reflect the demands of the very dynamic working environments of many organizations today and the rapidly changing context in which they are operating. This theme will be explored more in Chapter 4.

Activities of performance management

So, moving to the present day, what are the key activities typically forming part of performance management in organizations? When I ask line managers about the typical activities involved in performance management, generally their first response will be to mention the performance appraisal or review. It is true that for some the term performance management has become synonymous with the performance appraisal or performance review, but this is only a subset of the entire performance management process, a single technique used by many organizations to manage performance.

Typical activities coming under the term 'performance management' include: objective setting, feedback, the performance review/appraisal and development. A 2009 survey by the Chartered Institute of Personnel and Development (CIPD) found that the core activities of performance management were: performance appraisal, objective setting, regular feedback, regular reviews and assessment of development needs. These are certainly the key activities that students consistently tell me represent performance management in their organizations.

Such a range of activities can bring with it some tensions within the performance management process and particularly within the performance appraisal. There are activities that are quite clearly linked to making a judgement about an individual's performance, and others that are focused on development through identification of training needs or career plans. Much debate exists about how well these activities sit alongside each other. The issue is aggravated when judgement is closely aligned to financial reward. Some people will argue that any attempt to separate out a review of performance from any discussion about reward is very difficult to achieve. However, there is little doubt that some employees may be quite guarded about areas they need to improve on or develop, when they know that at the end of any discussion a number will be generated that is then linked to annual pay review or bonus.

Whilst there may be a fair degree of consistency in terms of the types of performance management activities that exist in many organizations today, the way these activities are carried out can vary considerably. The degree to which these activities add value, supporting the goals of the organization, can also vary considerably. This book will consider not only 'what' should be done in terms of performance management activities, but 'how' these activities can be carried out to deliver value for the organization.

The goals of performance management

For performance management processes to be successful, we need a clear idea of what we want them to achieve. A focus needs to be established with provision of clear criteria for success. This may sound obvious but not all organizations can clearly articulate the response to the question 'Why are we doing this?' Clarity around the goals and intended impact of performance management is really important in getting the buy-in of managers and employees. So a key question to be addressed is, once we have implemented our performance management processes, what outcomes will we expect to see? Clear goals are also essential if we are to evaluate the impact of performance management – a key activity when justifying the costs and time involved in any performance management process.

The goals of performance management will and should vary according to the specific circumstances of the organization; however, we can identify some generic elements that most performance management systems and processes should deliver.

Effective performance management should ensure that people:

- understand what is required of them, results and behaviours (inputs and outputs);
- understand how they contribute to the goals of the organization;
- are motivated to perform;
- have the skills and ability to deliver required performance levels;
- are supported by the organization in meeting what is expected of them;
- understand how they are performing (feedback);
- deliver the performance required;
- are rewarded appropriately (fairly) for their contribution.

In the last bullet point the term 'rewarded' should relate to 'total reward', so non-financial rewards such as recognition and development can form part of this area rather than just a focus purely on the financial transaction.

The IRS (2003) identified a variety of aims for performance management expressed by a variety of organizations:

- Empowering, motivating and rewarding employees to do (and for doing) their best. *Armstrong World Industries Inc*

- Focusing employees' tasks on the right things and doing them right. Aligning everyone's individual goals to the goals of the organization. *Eli Lilly & Co Ltd*

- Proactively managing and resourcing performance against agreed accountabilities and objectives. *ICI Paints*

- The process and behaviours by which managers manage the performance of their people to deliver a high-achieving organization. *Standard Chartered Bank*

- Maximizing the potential of individuals and teams to benefit themselves and the organization, focusing on achievement of their objectives. *West Bromwich Building Society* (as cited in Armstrong, 2006)

At a base level, performance management should at least be ensuring that people clearly understand what is required of them, that they are supported in achieving what is needed and that they are given regular feedback to enable them to continuously improve. Blanchard's *The One Minute Manager* (2011) reflected this very succinctly with his one-minute goals, praise and reprimands. I believe that in any job role there are three key questions an employee needs to have answers to:

- What do you/the organization expect of me?

- How am I doing?

- In the current workplace environment where future employability is key – how can I develop/improve?

Activity

Consider the three questions above in relation to your role in your organization. Write down your responses to the following questions:

- How easy do you find it to provide clear responses to these questions?

- Is your response based on your own perceptions or from concrete information discussed and agreed with your manager?

- If you have struggled to provide effective responses what can be done to enable you to be able to answer the questions effectively?

You may find it helpful to ask some of your colleagues whether they feel they are able to provide clear responses to these questions – and then see if there is a consistency in the responses.

Who is involved with performance management?

The simple answer to this is 'everyone' in your organization and increasingly other stakeholders who may not be part of the organization. A key question to ask is: Who has an interest in the performance of this individual or these individuals? In many organizations today, the manager charged with setting and agreeing objectives and conducting the performance appraisal of an employee may actually have little day-to-day or face-to-face contact with that employee. The employee may, for example, spend most of his or her time out at a client site and any evaluation of performance might be worthless without the involvement of someone from the client team. Let us consider then, the stakeholders in the performance management process.

I would suggest that the key stakeholders are the senior management team of the organization. Their commitment to and active involvement with performance management is widely identified as a critical success factor in any performance management process. For performance management to be effective, desired behaviours need to be 'role-modelled' by the senior management team if they are to stand any chance of being embedded further down the organization. I have had many discussions with line managers in exploring problems with performance management and they have said to me: 'How can I set objectives for my team when I haven't been set any myself?' This is a totally valid response and places any HR manager in a difficult position in terms of justifying their request. It highlights the problem that lack of commitment at the top of the organization will have significant consequences for commitment elsewhere.

In recent times performance management has shifted from a 'controlling' activity to one of partnership, where employer and employee share responsibility for delivering required levels of performance. The employee has a responsibility to play an active part in developing objectives and identifying the required performance to deliver against those objectives and to strive for continuous improvement. No longer is performance management something that is done to employees – they should be active not passive participants. To be active participants, employees (particularly more junior employees) will need organizational support to ensure they have the confidence and ability to do so.

The line manager has a key role supporting, enabling and creating an environment in which the employee is more likely to be motivated to perform. Performance management is fundamental to this. As with other areas of HRM, over recent times there has been a recognition that people management issues have to be driven and owned by line managers rather than the HR function. The research of Hutchinson and Purcell (2003) has shown the vital role that front-line managers have in people management. Performance management is a key delivery mechanism for line managers to drive performance through strong communication, support, and building trust and respect. Satisfaction with performance management processes, and appraisals in particular, rises significantly when line managers own the process and are truly engaged with it, rather than going through the motions with gritted teeth! In my experience, and those of many HR people I have worked with or taught over the years, the key challenge for HR professionals is getting the line manager on board with the performance management process. Armstrong (2006) summarizes this in a lovely term: 'HR proposes but the line disposes'. If the line managers are not committed to carrying out HRM activities then these activities will struggle to be achieved. This is where being able to identify some clear outputs or value from the performance management process is extremely important. If you were a busy line manager asked to do an appraisal in order only to tick a box, would it really be top of your list of priorities? Line management commitment to performance management becomes even more vital when we are moving to an approach requiring more regular meetings and dialogue between managers and those they manage.

So what, then, is the role for HR in performance management? There has been a perception historically that appraisal and performance management are the responsibility of the HR function. In the worst cases HR might be perceived to be in some kind of policing role, just ensuring that appraisals are completed and recorded, but with little thought to any added value. It is now largely agreed that whilst HR have a key role in performance management, it is not the sole responsibility of HR to make it happen.

If we take Ulrich and Brockbank's model of HRM roles (2005) – functional expert, employee advocate, strategic partner, human capital developer and HR leader – as a framework we can explore the role of HR in performance management. First, as functional expert HR can provide the knowledge and expertise of performance management. Using IT effectively to support performance management, HR should be able to advise on efficient and effective policies and procedures. They should then provide an effective framework within which performance can be effectively managed on an ongoing basis. In recent years there has been a steep rise in HR roles with a focus on data analytics. HR can have an important role here interpreting large quantities of data drawn from performance management processes to provide sound intelligence to inform HR and organizational decisions moving forward.

Second, as employee advocate HR can ensure that the voice of the employees is heard through the performance management processes and that employees are not only given a voice, but are given the support and development to enable them to be confident participants in the performance management process. Also as employee advocate, HR has a role to ensure the procedural and distributive fairness of performance management, which is discussed further at various points in this book. In the employee advocate role, HR can also identify any barriers to encouraging diversity that may exist within the performance management process and work with senior and line managers to remove these barriers.

Third, as strategic partner, HR has a role to work with the senior management team to ensure that performance management supports the strategic goals and values of the organization. This area is discussed in more detail in Chapter 3.

The role of human capital developer goes to the heart of performance management. Both through the design of processes and giving support to line managers and employees, HR has an important role in ensuring that there is a focus on development within performance management, to ensure through training and learning, coaching and career development that the workforce of the organization can develop the skill, knowledge and attitudes required to support the future success of the organization.

Finally, in the role of HR leader it is vital again that good practice in performance management is role-modelled. Some time ago I did some research with a large college of further education in south-east England. The HR director was able to contribute much value by providing a role model for performance management in the organization. She effectively managed the performance of her team, but also coached the senior management team to do the same for the programme managers and curriculum area leaders in the college.

When there needs to be involvement in performance management by individuals outside the organization such as clients, careful consideration needs to be given to how this can work most effectively. It may simply mean gathering feedback from clients on an individual, or it could mean a client undertaking the full appraisal of an individual. Strong communication and support from the organization and HR will be a key underlying requirement here. It is important that there is consistency in approach.

It is important to recognize that all these potential stakeholders in the performance management process may have different perspectives on and interests in the process. For example, your senior management team is likely to be focused on how performance management will be supporting the achievement of organization goals. The line managers are likely to be more concerned with day-to-day operational effectiveness and also dealing with any areas of underperformance. The financial director is likely to be more focused on areas such as reward strategy and its link to performance management, and also on maximizing profitability and limiting costs. The HR department will be concerned with the business requirements for performance management, but also is likely to be concerned with the implementation of good practice and ensuring that there is fairness and consistency of approach across the organization. Individual employees are likely to be focused on their own roles, how they are rewarded, and opportunities to grow and develop. These varying perspectives and interests will create challenges in the formation and implementation of any performance management process. It is important to identify the perspectives and interests of the various stakeholders in the performance management process in order to maximize engagement.

Approaches to performance management

Organizations can take a variety of approaches to managing performance. The approach taken will be heavily influenced by such factors as the type of organization (sector, size, culture) and the pervasive management style. Taylor (2008) identifies two distinct perspectives associated with different uses of performance management in organizations. First, the standards-orientated approach where the emphasis is on ensuring compliance to standards. Performance management processes will focus on clearly defined objectives for all and close monitoring of performance against those standards. Another key area in this approach will be managing underperformance where employees are not meeting the required standards. There is an important role for the line manager here in identifying underperformance at an early stage, communicating this to the employee and, with the employee, identifying the most effective approach to bring performance up to the required standard. This approach has been linked to a transactional leadership style in which, depending on whether the required performance is met, either a 'reward' or 'punishment' will follow.

The second approach that Taylor (2008) identifies is that of the 'excellence-orientated approach'. Here the focus of performance management is on striving for excellence, continuous improvement and development.

There isn't a 'ceiling' of objectives to be met, but a sky where individuals are encouraged to reach out for the highest level of performance they can. The emphasis here for performance management is to create an environment where individuals are motivated to perform, committed to achieving excellence, and equipped with the skills and knowledge to deliver that excellence. This approach has been linked to the transformational style of leadership. Transformational leaders provide a clear vision and empower employees to meet higher standards. There is a shift in emphasis here from control to commitment.

There is some debate as to how easily these two approaches can co-exist. How easy is it, for example, for people to strive for excellence – which often requires a degree of creativity, or an element of risk-taking – against a backdrop of high levels of control and structure? Arguably this has been a long-standing problem for performance management processes that typically incorporate elements of control through the monitoring and evaluation of performance whilst aiming to develop high levels of organization commitment. Certainly for many of the organizations I have come into contact with, both of these approaches can be found in existence in the same organization and it may be more of an issue of emphasis.

Another interesting approach to performance management is that of a strengths-based approach. This involves performance management focusing on people's strengths rather than on their weaknesses when seeking to improve their performance. Instead of trying to develop areas in which an individual may never be very effective, this approach encourages identifying what people do well and then finding them more opportunities to use the skills and knowledge they have in those areas. Initial take-up of this approach was slow and there was some cynicism about the practicality of such an approach. However, more recently there has been a growth in adoption of this approach by organizations. Recent research conducted by the CIPD in partnership with the civil service (CIPD, 2017c) focused on strengths-based performance conversations. If you are aiming for more frequent, strengths-based performance conversations in your organization, this interesting recent research highlights the importance of training particularly for line managers, supporting HR policies and resources and a backdrop of wider communication.

DIAGNOSTIC QUESTIONNAIRE

To enable you to be able to get the best use from this book you should aim to find out as much as you can about performance management in your organization. To start you off on that process I have identified below a few questions to provide a base for your exploration of performance management. You may find it helpful to ask a range of people in your organization for their views on the questions outlined below (for example a senior manager, a financial manager, a line manager, a member of the HR department). We have discussed the fact that the various stakeholders in performance management may have different perspectives and interests in performance management activity. So by asking a range of individuals, this may enable you to highlight differences or similarities/trends in responses. You can then build a picture of both the reality and the perceptions of performance management in your organization.

Taking this activity forward, you could also use these questions to find out about performance management in other organizations. The importance and value of benchmarking is explored in the final chapter of this book, and whilst another organization's approach to performance management might not be the right one for yours, it is very useful to learn about various approaches in coming to an informed decision about what approach and activities would work and add value in your organization.

TABLE 1.1 Exploring performance management in your organization

What activities form part of performance management in your organization?
Consider the elements of performance management identified in the 'historical context' section of this chapter. Which of the stages of the development of performance management can you identify in your organization's approach?

(continued)

TABLE 1.1 *(Continued)*

What are the goals of performance management in your organization?
What should the outputs be? What are the criteria for success?
Who is involved in performance management in your organization? Who are the key stakeholders in the process?
To what degree do line managers 'own' the performance management process in your organization?
What approach does your organization take to performance management? For example, is it more standards-orientated or excellence-orientated in nature?
Could a strengths-based approach work in your organization? Justify your response.

This chapter has aimed to equip you with a good understanding of what is meant by performance management and should have enabled you to start to explore performance management within your own organization. To start you thinking about some of the significant themes in performance management, given below is an overview of an interview I conducted with Martin Eves, HR and Operations Director of QiO Technologies Ltd. Martin leads the development of the Human Capital, Finance, IT and Legal functions of the organization. He has held senior HR roles for Shell, BOC Gases, PepsiCo and Nestlé and more recently with Vertu and Kronos. Drawing on his extensive experience in the HR field I asked him what he believed were some of the key factors in delivering effective performance in the workplace. He identified four key areas, as shown here.

The HR director's viewpoint

There is a simple truth that I have witnessed in the organizations that I have worked in: when managers set a clear direction with targets and engage with their work group, the energy that is created is infectious. This is performance management.

Many tools exist to help create and sustain this energy and each employee will respond differently to different stimuli. All tools will have an impact; however, only the right choice will create the required change. The choice of tool has to take into consideration the local context – and this is where a 'one-size approach' rarely fits. A manager has received the 'right' to lead and change behaviour; in considering how to improve the performance of his or her employee(s), he or she needs to understand the 'context' by asking why they behave as they do. What value do they bring? How, as part of a team, can that value be enhanced further?

The value of the employee

All employees can add value. Senior managers have been given the responsibility to identify and enhance that value. Although individual development is important, how that employee assimilates with the team and the culture is also a senior manager's responsibility; indeed success here often drives greater performance and results.

Employee resignation can be for a variety of reasons; however, it is usually when the relationship breaks down between an employee and a senior manager. It is often useful to reflect on whether the senior manager really has identified the value the employee can add. It is interesting to note that in most cases employees leave senior managers, especially those managers who have not been able to harness that employee's value – rarely do employees leave companies.

The importance of shared purpose

Employees need to understand the overall purpose of the organization, their department and their role and how they combine to contribute. Whether the company provides a service or sells a product, it is important that there is a shared understanding of what the organization is trying to achieve.

Confidence in the purpose should cascade through the organization. Senior management has an important role to play here in communicating the purpose and building confidence throughout the organization; this helps deliver superior organizational performance.

This shared purpose creates synergistic performance that can be contagious, creative and powerful. Many organizations underestimate the power of a coherent single simple truth that everyone can align behind.

Fit performance management to the context

It's not just about alignment to the goals of the organization; it is important that performance management suits the organizational context.

For example, you would intuitively think that a sales consultant who is solely incentivized to sell would generate the best sales results. This, though, is too general and does not take the context into consideration. If you think of a luxury car showroom where customer experience is fundamental to the sale, you would want to incentivize the team to create the right environment – this will actually increase sales. Get this wrong and you end up with a sales team that attacks every person who enters the showroom – in the hope of closing the few deals that arrive each week.

Getting the reward and recognition component right will increase sales or customer service: the next time you enter a sales room or are talking to a call centre see if you can see how they are incentivized – it is often quite transparent.

Managing expectations

Likewise, the management of expectations will also have a strong impact on employee performance. Through an annual appraisal process a large multinational I worked with had a process that reviewed where an employee was reasonably expected to aspire to in the organization's grading structure. Those with high potential were pulled through the organization by their higher potential rating, accelerating them through the organizational structure. The potential was assessed each year, reconfirming or realigning the employees' rating level. This process had a significant impact on the employees' behaviour: those advised of high potential behaved differently to those who were advised of lower potential. This created a self-fulfilling context and 'managed' the expectations of employees across all functions of the organization.

In isolation, any of these elements badly managed can destroy the foundations of good employee performance management. Taking the time to understand your employees, creating synergy through a shared purpose, having an appreciation for the operational context and professionally managing expectations will ensure a high performance culture.

These themes will be explored in greater depth as you work through this book.

The next chapter will look at why performance management is important and what benefits effective performance management has for organizations. Understanding and communicating the value that effective performance management can bring is essential in gaining commitment to the performance management process.

02 Why is it important?

Delivering performance

Delivering effective performance is at the heart of all we do in HRM. With people being a major part of an organization's operating costs, it is vital that they are adding value rather than just being an overhead. As discussed in the previous chapter, now more than ever it is vital that we maximize the performance of those we employ. When working well, performance management should help to ensure that people are adding value through being effective (focused on the right things) and efficient (carrying out their roles in the best way possible). Performance management should also respect and embed factors that support employee well-being. Well, happy employees are more likely to deliver good performance outcomes than those whose well-being is negatively impacted at work. Performance management should provide a focus and a framework whereby organizations and managers can create an environment where human resources can contribute and grow that contribution over time.

Delivering performance to manage and create change

Organizations have always had to manage and create change, but it is the growing pace of change that is presenting particular challenges for organizations today. Performance management is vital to enable organizations not only to respond to change, but ideally to be proactive in identifying and creating change. Change can only happen in organizations when people are equipped with the skills, knowledge and attitude required. One of the biggest barriers to change is fear – and this can be broken down through the performance management process.

Scenario

A team of hotel receptionists in a large hotel in London have been working to a fairly static job description over the last few years. The core of their job has been dealing with booking enquiries over the phone and booking in and checking out guests. Increasing competition has resulted in a drop in bookings over the last 12–18 months and part of the manager's response has been to get the receptionists to take on a more proactive role in dealing with customer enquiries. They have been given the option to make special offers and present seasonal deals to potential guests within certain guidelines. Whilst some of the team will be delighted at this opportunity for greater autonomy within the role, for some of the reception team this change will present a daunting prospect. They will have been very comfortable with an ordered, black-and-white structure of costs. The challenge of a more sales-orientated approach may make some of the receptionists feel nervous and they may lack the confidence to move forward. Others may see the change as managers offloading more work and responsibility on them with no benefit to them. Some things performance management can do here are:

- Provide a reason for change – by aligning the change in the receptionists' job role to the wider needs of the organization the receptionists can see a purpose and a value to change.

- Provide clear objectives – identifying clearly what should be achieved is particularly important here, explaining how it should be achieved in terms of the new behaviours the hotel is looking for, such as 'selling'.

- Provide training/development – by whatever intervention, training or coaching provides the receptionists with the supporting knowledge and skills necessary to meet the new requirements of the job role. This will nurture confidence, a vital ingredient for effective performance.

- Provide feedback – when individuals start to respond to a need for change it is really important that they receive early and prompt feedback to know how they are doing. As explored in greater depth in the next section, our receptionists will be more motivated to respond to the requirement for change when they know that they have the ability to respond and are starting to achieve the requirements of the job. Where they are struggling, provide constructive feedback to help them identify how they can improve their performance moving forward.

- Consider some form of reward or recognition for this change in responsibilities (this doesn't have to be financial – it could be a 'receptionist of the month' award, recognizing success with the new responsibilities).

The above scenario takes a small issue and group within an organization, but some of the key elements of performance management discussed here are likely to contribute positively in many situations where change is required.

It is not only the response to change, however, that performance management can support. It can help to provide employees with a confidence and curiosity to identify opportunities for change. Here are some examples of how performance management can support this:

- Instilling a clear understanding of the goals of the organization and the context in which it operates, and communicating how the organization is doing. (If employees cannot see beyond their role they may have limited knowledge by which to grow their role, or contribute beyond their role.)

- Nurturing skills and behaviours that deliver flexibility, creativity and innovation (through objective setting, use of competency frameworks, learning and development interventions and providing the autonomy to explore).

- Using feedback to grow, develop and encourage rather than blame (change often involves an element of risk-taking; this is unlikely to be possible in an organization where there is blame culture and low tolerance of mistakes).

Motivation

To deliver effective performance, employees need to be motivated to perform. Purcell *et al* (2003) proposed a model that linked an employee's ability, motivation and opportunity (AMO) to organizational performance. The AMO model of performance states that employees are likely to perform well and use their discretion in carrying out their roles when they have:

A – the Ability to perform because they have the appropriate skills and knowledge to carry out the role;

M – the Motivation to perform because they want to do so;

O – the Opportunity to perform because their role is designed and supported (through effective resourcing) in such a way as to enable them
to do so.

All three of these elements are important in delivering effective performance. For example, you may have a very able employee in a role that has
been designed well for them to demonstrate their knowledge and skill set;
however, if for whatever reason they are not motivated to perform then you
will not get the performance you are looking for.

Whilst we can create an environment where employees feel compelled to
deliver the performance required, for legal and ethical reasons and for the
long-term good of the employment relationship this is not an ideal scenario.
Sustainable performance is not built on coercion. We need employees who
want to perform, who want to deliver the required performance. We cannot
force them to be motivated, but we can create an environment in which they
are more likely to be motivated to perform. Our performance management
processes are crucial in creating that environment.

It is helpful to explore some of the theories of motivation in order to
consider how performance management processes can create an environment where people are more likely to be motivated to perform. There are
a huge range of theories of motivation, many of which have relevance for
performance management. However, having explored motivation with
my students over many years, I have found that there are three theories in
particular that have a strong relevance to performance management:

- goal-setting theory;
- expectancy theory;
- equity theory.

Goal-setting theory is based on the belief in a causal link between a person's
goals and their behaviour, and on the idea that people are likely to be motivated
by being set challenging goals. The word 'challenging' is very important
here. It is not enough to be given an objective to achieve at work. If that
objective is something that does not stretch us, does not require us to put
in any effort or make good utilization of our skill and knowledge base,
it is unlikely to motivate. The studies of Locke (1968) argued that more
difficult and specific goals result in higher levels of performance than easy
ones. Performance management should provide individuals with clearly
defined, understood and challenging objectives. Goals set should be challenging, but should also be realistic. Goals that are too difficult, or that
are felt to be beyond the control of the employee, can lead to stress and
underperformance – so a careful balance is needed. It is also important

that the employee receives regular, timely feedback on progress against the goals. This provides reassurance that their efforts are leading them in the right direction, or information that they can then use to amend behaviour if required. To ensure feedback is objective, it is important that goals are clear and capable of objective measurement.

Expectancy theories of motivation work on the basis that individuals will be motivated to perform if they see a valuable outcome to that performance. Most expectancy theories are based around the work of Vroom, Porter and Lawler and focus on a relationship between effort, effective performance and rewards that are valued. Let's look at this in relation to a short case study.

CASE STUDY

Catherine is an administrator in a small marketing company. She is having her annual appraisal with her manager and her objectives for the next six months are being set. Catherine's manager is seeking her agreement to the following objective: review the current recruitment methods used by the company and make recommendations to improve the effectiveness and efficiency of recruitment by X date.

There is no HR function in the company and HR does not currently come within Catherine's job description. If you were Catherine, consider what might your thought process be at this point: 1) Given my current workload, do I have the capacity to deliver this in the time frame required? 2) Do I have the skills and knowledge required to achieve this task?

Here Catherine is assessing whether, given a reasonable amount of effort, this task is achievable. She might also be considering the following: 1) If I deliver against this objective what is the likely reward for my effort? 2) Is this reward worth the effort I am expending on the objective?

Here she is trying to identify a link between effort and reward. That reward doesn't have to be financial, it could be a promotion, more responsibility, a sense of achievement, career development, or recognition/approval from her manager. The important thing here is that she perceives a link between her effort and a reward in that the reward is something of value to her.

Catherine might feel she has little choice but to agree to this objective, but if she feels that this is an objective that is both achievable and of value to her, she will be more likely to be motivated to perform. If she has the ability and knowledge, as well as the motivation to perform, we are likely to get a good level of performance from Catherine against this objective. However, if Catherine is already snowed under with work, sees this as job enlargement with no perceived reward, or a reward that has little value to her given the effort required, we are unlikely to have a motivated administrator!

The employment relationship is an exchange. I am bringing my knowledge, skills, experience and effort to your organization and in return you are going to give me some kind of a reward for those things. Equity theories of motivation look closely at that exchange and evaluate its fairness. When the exchange is perceived to be fair there is a greater likelihood of the employee being motivated to perform. The backdrop to this is the concept of 'distributive justice' – the sense of fairness in distribution of reward. Do we perceive a sense of fairness between what we are required to put in to carrying out our jobs (inputs) and what we are getting out of the job (outputs)? Let's return to our administrator, Catherine, at this point.

Scenario

Catherine has had a tough month. She is having a well-deserved glass of wine with her friends and they are discussing their jobs. Catherine tells her friends she has had to work long hours over the last few months to stay on top of the objectives she has been set. She envies her friends who have fairly fixed 9–5 jobs, leaving lots of time for other interests. However, as the evening progresses she finds herself enthusiastically telling her friends about what she is learning at work, how valued her manager makes her feel and the coaching she is being given to support her with her long-term aim of moving into an HRM role. Catherine goes home feeling good about her job. She might work hard, but she enjoys her work, is learning and can see opportunities to grow and develop.

Catherine has been weighing up the exchange in the employment relationship. She has been looking at what she is putting into her job in terms of effort, hours, etc (the inputs) and comparing it with what she is getting out of the job in terms of enjoyment, challenge, growth, recognition etc (outputs). She perceives 'the deal' to be a fair one. Because of this she is likely to be motivated to perform.

Equity theory extends beyond the exchange between employer and employee. Equity theory also involves a thought process in which we consider the nature of our 'exchange', the balance of input and output, with a referent group; for example, other individuals who carry out similar roles in the organization. We might be fairly happy with the nature of our own personal exchange with the organization; however, we start to notice that other employees are not working nearly so hard, or delivering anywhere near the same level of performance, but are receiving the same rewards as us (outputs). It may be that we feel we are carrying other members of the team in this situation, sometimes referred to as 'the sucker effect'. Thus we may decide to reduce our efforts as there is no apparent reward for our hard work and others are just riding off the back of it. Or perhaps we perceive other employees delivering the same level of performance as us, but become aware that they are receiving much greater rewards. In this position we start to feel a sense of injustice and once again our motivation to perform may decline. Here the concepts of procedural justice and interactional justice (how those procedures are implemented and the outcomes) are relevant. Are fair procedures for managing performance in place? Are they used fairly by the line managers required to apply them? Do they result in fair outcomes?

Fair processes, equitable and consistent treatment in performance management processes, are more likely to create an environment where employees are motivated to perform. Where processes do not lead to fair outcomes, or there is a perception of inequitable treatment or favouritism, motivation to perform may well decline. The greater the perceived inequity in 'the deal', the greater the potential for a negative impact on employee behaviour in the workplace. For example, a sense of inequity or unfairness may lead to a lack of co-operation, or rising absence levels, or a rise in conflict such as grievances and, in the worst scenario, employees may vote with their feet and leave the organization.

The psychological contract

The employment contract provides a formal, legal agreement between employer and employee and sets boundaries in which the employment relationship should be conducted. Performance management processes need to work in accordance with and support of the employment contract, but they also have a key role in maintaining the health of the psychological contract.

The concept of the psychological contract has strong links to the equity theory we have just been exploring and is fundamentally about the nature of the exchange relationship between employee and employer. There are many varying definitions of the psychological contract, but the work of Rousseau (1998) best encapsulates the concept for me. It is concerned with an individual's subjective beliefs that are shaped by the organization, regarding the terms of the exchange in the employment relationship. It is about expectations of the employee and, for some theorists, the expectations of the employer in terms of what each party should expect from the employment relationship. Despite the fact that the psychological contract is unwritten, Rousseau saw the contract as having a promissory element. The employee perceives that promises have been made in terms of what the employment relationship will deliver. This element of promise gives the contract considerable power to influence the health of the employment relationship. For example, if you have a vague expectation that the employment relationship will deliver something and that expectation is not met, this may not have a significant impact on your attitude to your employer or the way you behave in the workplace. However, if you feel a promise has been made to you and that promise has not been met, then that is much more likely to lead to negativity in attitude and even worse in behavioural outcomes. Performance management processes have a vital role in enabling the ongoing and two-way communication of expectations in the employment relationship.

The terms 'mutuality' and 'reciprocity' are often used in relation to a healthy psychological contract. In a healthy contract, both parties clearly understand the nature of the exchange in the employment relationship and both parties feel that the perceived obligations in the exchange are being met. Conversely, where there is a sense that obligations are not being met there may be a breach of the psychological contract. It is likely that during our employment with an organization, particularly when we are employed over a significant period of time, we may at some point perceive that our psychological contract has been breached. For example, maybe there has been a misunderstanding in communication between you and your manager and you feel aggrieved that a commitment has not been met. This isn't necessarily going to cause significant damage to your employment relationship; however, if you perceive that regular breaches are occurring, a fundamental prop to a healthy working relationship starts to erode – trust! In our working relationships, just as with other relationships in our lives, once trust is lost it is hard to regain or rebuild. Clear, transparent, regular communication in the performance management process will help avoid any confusion over expectations and avoid breach and violation of the psychological contract.

The research of Guest and Conway (1997) has shown the importance of a healthy psychological contract in the management of the employment relationship. A healthy contract is one where there is perceived fairness, high levels of trust and a perception that both parties are getting what they should from the employment relationship. When the contract is healthy, employees are more likely to have positive attitudes towards their employing organization, demonstrated in valuable behaviours and valuable performance outcomes.

The psychological contract during change

A key part of managing performance is communicating the expectations of the employer and outlining what the employee should expect in return. This process starts during the recruitment and selection process when both parties form an understanding of how the employment relationship is going to work. This is sometimes referred to as giving a realistic job preview, or 'RJP'. However, even if the process at the commencement of the employment relationship works effectively, during the continuance of the employment relationship things are very likely to change. As discussed above, organizations today are having to respond to a growing pace of change and, as a result of those changes, the nature of the psychological contract may need to change. An expectation an employee had on commencement of their employment with an organization may no longer be able to be met by the organization. A very topical example of this would be a pension arrangement (particularly evidenced in the public sector recently), but it might be an issue such as the entitlement to a staff discount, or a parking space in the company car park. Some of these issues clearly have legal implications that are present in the employment contract and are likely to be documented, but this will not be the case for all issues within the psychological contract.

A required change in expectations always has the potential to lead to a negative impact on the attitude and, in turn, the behaviour of employees, but any damage can be limited through discussion and dialogue about the reasons for any change. Whilst a breach of contract may occur, a violation where trust is lost can hopefully be avoided and a healthy psychological contract maintained. Performance management has a clear function in providing a forum for the discussion of the need for change and a resetting of expectations.

Stiles *et al* (1997) emphasize the important link between performance management and the state of the psychological contract: 'performance management processes play a key role in creating the framework in which the psychological contract is determined'. Processes such as objective setting, feedback and ongoing two-way communication within performance management can support the maintenance of a healthy contract, manage expectations effectively and support required change.

The employer brand

Despite the challenging economic times we are living in, there is still much competition between organizations to attract the most talented employees. The employer brand has been shown to have a vital role in the attraction and retention of employees, and performance management forms a key part of the delivery of a strong, positive employer brand. When communicated effectively the employer brand provides a proposition for the employment relationship in an organization. It aims to communicate what the experience of working for an organization will be like, and as with branding in other types of marketing – we are *selling* here. The sell needs to be targeted, as not all organizations' environments suit all potential employees. Identifying the essence of why your most talented people enjoy working for the organization is important here. However, communication of excellence in your HR practices provides a strong underlying basis for your brand. Communicating how your performance management processes create an environment where individuals can develop and achieve will strengthen your employer brand. In a world where we no longer have an expectation of a job for life, identifying employers that will invest in us, updating our skills and knowledge so we remain employable, is very important.

For over 15 years now Best Companies and the *Sunday Times* have produced the 'Best Companies to Work For' list by surveying employees. The survey attracts wide interest from employers and employees alike, providing a 'kite mark' of good practice, as evidenced by the employees themselves. Those companies achieving well in these surveys have evidenced positive impact on their ability to attract employees to their workplaces. Whilst many of the criteria used in this survey can be linked to performance management, two in particular have strong relevance. First, **personal growth** examines whether people feel challenged by their jobs, whether their skills are being utilized and their perceived opportunities for advancement. As we shall explore later in more depth, performance management provides a forum within which stretching objectives can be set, skill can be applied and opportunities for growth identified. Second, **my manager** measures whether people feel supported, trusted and cared for by their immediate manager. As discussed in Chapter 1, the line manager has a vital role in delivering effective performance management of employees. Whilst managing performance, if line managers can deliver clarity in objectives, open, constructive and development feedback, and support through activities such as coaching – they are more likely to have high performing and engaged employees.

Judith Leary-Joyce (2004) has explored factors that make organizations places where people want to do great work. Two areas she examines have strong linkage to performance management. First, 'taking responsibility and providing support'. Performance management when delivered effectively can provide a framework whereby employees can be given autonomy, enabling them to develop and grow within a supportive environment. Support is important here, because if we are given too much responsibility without the skills, knowledge and confidence to manage it this may well result in high levels of stress. The second area is 'building a sense of belonging'. Performance management when delivered effectively can engender a sense of 'being part' of an organization rather than just 'working for' an organization. A clear understanding of contribution, a sense that the contribution is valued by the organization and peers, and that there is fairness in the employment relationship are vital elements of this.

The legal and ethical framework

Effective performance management can help ensure that an organization stays within the law and is able to demonstrate a strong ethical stance to managing people. The heroic, macho style of leadership popular in the 1990s has been largely replaced with a hunger for authentic leadership – leaders who operate ethically, honestly and transparently. Employees need to trust those who lead them and this is more likely to happen where there is a sense of transparency, and a consistent commitment to core values.

The ethical backdrop

Back in 2008, the world was faced with one of the biggest financial crises since the Great Depression of the 1930s. Unethical business practices came to light; the dangers of short-term greed versus a focus on long-term sustainable performance. Since that time there has been a much greater focus on ethical business practices. Linked to this has been a hunger for transparency in the world of work, including between workers and organizations.

The CIPD viewpoint is outlined in their Fact Sheet *Business Ethics and the Role of HR* (2017a):

> We believe that work can and should be a force for good, for everyone involved in the world of work. Because when work is good, people are more likely to be happy and fulfilled, businesses are more likely to be productive and profitable, and communities are more likely to flourish.

The CIPD's new Professional Standards Framework includes a strong focus on ethics in the professional people management and development practices. 'HR professionals play a central role in supporting a workplace culture where the motivation for "doing the right thing" is because it's the right thing to do. Sometimes, that may mean compromising performance in the short term. Ethical businesses support that, because of the benefits in the long-term' (CIPD, 2017a). Ethics can and should be integrated into the performance management process.

Most organizations will have some core values that underpin their work. Sometimes these will be clearly articulated and communicated, sometimes less so, but a sense of what these values are comes through in the culture of the organization. For those values to come to life, it is vital that they are truly role-modelled from the top of the organization and throughout. Any gap between rhetoric and reality may well lead to a disillusionment and related lack of commitment to those values and impact on trust within the organization.

When agreeing performance expectations, it is important that upholding company values form part of those expectations. This is most likely to be captured in relation to behavioural expectations. This is explored further in Chapter 6 but it is important to highlight here that a focus purely on end results and not on how people get to those results runs the risk of unethical and or short-termist approaches that may be harmful to the organization, employees and wider stakeholders.

A core element of ethical behaviour is honesty and transparency, and this should be embedded firmly in performance practices; transparency in expectations, transparency of feedback and also in any assessment outcomes. There should be transparency in reward practices, so there is complete clarity in terms of how performance links to reward. Transparency on both sides of the employment relationship is much more likely to create and support an environment of trust. This is really important for performance management for where there is an environment of trust, people are much more likely to knowledge share, which we know has such a key role in delivering effective performance, saving time, building capability and driving innovation.

Activity

- Go onto the CIPD website and review the CIPD Code of Professional Conduct. This is a set of standards and behaviours that all member of the professional body should adhere to. There is much here that has relevance to all involved with managing people in organizations. How well does your organization reflect the standards and behaviour outlined here?

- Your organization or profession may well have a similar Code of Conduct. Review the content. Does this reflect how people operate in your organization, or is there a gap between the expectation and reality?

- Use your reflections to develop some Action Steps for your organization (or area) moving forward.
  - What can be done to close any gaps moving forward? (Greater communication, training and development, or more role-modelling from organization leaders for example.)
  - What actions should be prioritized to ensure practice matches the intention?

Organizations must also work within a framework of employment law and within an ever-changing political environment. Claims brought against organizations to employment tribunals can be very costly in terms of time, money and the reputation of the organization. Indeed the reputation element is perhaps the most important. A reputation as a good employer can take a considerable time to build up, but very little time to damage or destroy.

The legal backdrop

This book is not the place for an in-depth discussion of employment law (for this, see the specific title in the HR Fundamentals series, *Employment Law*); however, it is important to reflect on the fact that many decisions in employment tribunals have been made in the light of a close evaluation of the organization's performance management practices. It is not sufficient to demonstrate that these practices exist: demonstrating how they are implemented fairly is vitally important in ensuring the organization operates within the framework of employment law. Much of the current legislation that governs the employment relationship links back to the concepts of 'natural justice' and procedural fairness. The principles of natural justice have emerged from social norms and case law, and are associated with the concept of fairness, equity and transparency.

Performance management has a clear role in providing clarity in terms of what is expected from employees, both in terms of behaviour and results. Without that clarity how can employees be expected to deliver what the organization needs – and surely it is unreasonable to take action against an employee for underperformance when a lack of clarity exists? Employees are entitled to be supplied with knowledge of the standards or behaviour expected so that they understand fully what they need to achieve and how they need to behave in the workplace.

Performance management also has an important role in providing employees with the opportunity and support to improve their performance. Both my own experiences and the experiences that many HR professionals have shared with me support the occurrence in many organizations of the scenario below.

Scenario

A line manager bursts into the HR manager's office...

Line manager: 'That's it. I have had it up to here with Harry. He's messed up once too often – I want him out of here as soon as possible!'

The HR manager attempts to calm the line manager down and starts to ask some questions.

'What documented evidence do you have to demonstrate that this is a pattern of underperformance?' 'What did the last appraisal say?' 'How have you communicated this underperformance to Harry?' 'What support have you given Harry to improve his performance?'

Surprise, surprise, there is little evidence to support any kind of action against Harry. If an appraisal has been done at all, the HR manager may well find that to avoid confrontation, Harry has been middle-graded with 'satisfactory' or 'acceptable performance' rather than anything to indicate underperformance. When confronted about his underperformance, Harry looks confused and says he knows his manager isn't that keen on him and blows up at him occasionally, but he has no clear understanding of where he is failing and what he needs to do to improve.

Robust performance management processes ensure that if it is necessary to move into any formal, disciplinary action against the employee, then there is a sound, fair basis on which to proceed. Disciplinary action should be the last resort when performance management processes have been exhausted. Unfair dismissal claims can result where managers have not followed fair procedures in managing underperformance and taking disciplinary action, or when the organization cannot show through effective documentary evidence that fair procedures had been followed.

Effective performance management also helps ensure that organizations are less exposed to any claims relating to discrimination. Organizations should ensure that there are consistent review criteria in place and ensure that managers follow these criteria and that any evaluation processes are based on sound evidence. Consistent, fair, transparent processes in managing performance will help ensure that no individuals or groups are unfairly disadvantaged and will also support diversity. When performance management procedures are perceived as fair, any outcomes are more likely to be accepted. Fair process deeply impacts on the attitude and behaviour of employees and are more likely to lead to positive performance outcomes and trust in the employment relationship.

Another area of employment law linked to the performance management process is that of equal pay claims. Where performance management is linked to rewards such as pay increases, performance-related pay and discretionary bonuses, it is vitally important that any difference in reward outcome is based on fair, objective criteria.

To avoid exposure to bullying, harassment or victimization claims it is vital that line managers are given support and training in carrying out performance management. Employees should feel that their performance is being managed fairly and understand how they can raise concerns if they do not feel the process or decisions made are fair, making use of the company grievance process if necessary.

Record-keeping is an essential part of the performance management processes and particularly important in dealing with underperformance. It is important that the information held about an individual's performance in the job adheres to the requirement of data protection legislation. Consideration needs to be given to such issues as: what information is held on an individual, how it is held and for how long. Also, careful consideration should be given as to who will access the information. As with other areas of personnel data, employees should be clear on what information will be held on their records, how it is obtained and processed, and for what purpose it will be used. Individuals have rights under the Data Protection Act (2003) and General

Data Protection Regulations (2018). This includes the right to have access to the information you hold on them, to understand how it was obtained and processed, and who has access to the data. The Information Commissioner's Office can be contacted by employees with a complaint in this area.

In some organizations the backdrop of complex employment law makes managers risk-averse and pushes them towards middle marking of employees rather than managing poor performance. It is very important that managers are trained and supported in performance management and managing underperformance in order to ensure that the organization operates ethically and within the law.

Employee well-being at work

In recent years there has been a growing interest in employee well-being and growing evidence to suggest that promoting employee well-being is good for organizations as well as the individuals who work for them. Indeed, the UK government has recognized the importance of promoting health and well-being at work. A recent report published on the BIS website (2014) explores the link between work well-being and workplace performance. This report uses the term 'subjective well-being' (SWB): 'the various evaluations, positive and negative, that people make of their lives'. Factors influencing SWB at work include: autonomy over how employees do their job, variety in the work, clarity over what is expected of them and opportunities to use and develop skills, all of which have a strong alignment to performance management activities. The report outlines findings for policy makers and employers, the key message being 'there is a prima facie case for employers to consider investing in the well-being of their employees on the basis of the likely performance benefits'. The report argues that there are good reasons to expect employees with higher SWB to perform better in their jobs. Performance management carried out well has the potential to have a really positive impact on employee well-being.

Performance management and well-being: an interview with Professor Sir Cary Cooper held on 18 January 2018

Professor Cooper is 50th Anniversary Professor of Organizational Psychology & Health at ALLIANCE Manchester Business School, University of Manchester, President of the CIPD and co-founder of Robertson Cooper. He is recognized as a world-leading expert on well-being.

Why do you think there seems to be a much greater focus on well-being in the workplace over recent years?

I think a key factor here was the recession, which lasted a long time and changed the psychological contract between employer and employee. The recession that had a massive impact on employees' sense of job security. Organizations were trying to deliver more with less people, leading to people being more micro-managed to get the maximum output. The nature of work changed significantly during this time with the concept of jobs for life becoming a thing of the past. I spoke at a CPD conference recently to an audience of about 200 people and only a dozen people raised their hand when I asked 'Who would say that they had a secure and permanent job?' Less secure employment, more part-time work, short-term contracts and the growth of the gig economy has led to a situation where many perceive the psychological contract with their employing organization to be broken. Much is expected from workers with not always much given back in return.

So how does this link to the focus on well-being? Well, I asked a senior HR person in the finance sector 'Why all of a sudden is everyone in your sector looking at creating a culture of well-being, promoting flexible working and training line managers to support this?' His response was 'Regrettable Turnover'. They had lost so many people during the recession and beyond that they had become so lean and mean that they couldn't afford to lose anyone else. The drive towards a well-being culture had a clear aim to attract and retain talent.

A second factor is sickness absence. During the recession, sickness absence actually straight-lined or went down, but presenteeism went up. Significant job losses meant that individuals were worried about job security if they didn't turn up to work. Everyone thinks a focus on well-being is linked to absence, but the anxiety and depression caused by presenteeism also had a clear impact on productivity and talent retention. Organizations, particularly those who had the resource of occupational health, could increasingly see a clear link between well-being, productivity and retention of talent.

What role can HR have in getting support behind well-being initiatives, particularly from line managers?

HR has a role, in conjunction with occupational health, to develop a strategic well-being architecture for their organization. The exact nature of that will depend on the organization; different contexts will require a focus on different areas, but there are some key themes to consider.

Firstly, and I would say most importantly, is the role of the line manager. Line managers need to be socially skilled, to have or develop their emotional intelligence (EQ). HR need to ensure training is available for those who manage others and ensure that those who are untrainable are not in a manager role. Just because someone has great technical expertise, it doesn't mean they are right for a 'people management' role. Another factor in this is ensuring that EQ skill is assessed alongside other criteria in the recruitment and selection of future line managers. Alongside the essential technical capability, can they manage human beings? Are they emotionally sensitive? This is critical now we are out of the recession, and people are more mobile in their careers. For example, EQ will help managers identify employees who may be suffering from anxiety and depression, and the manager can find support systems to manage this. Emotionally intelligent line managers will be in a stronger position to motivate and retain staff as well, in difficult and challenging times.

The effective provision of flexible working arrangements is another important consideration, as is expecting a reasonable number of hours in a typical working week. Germany is one of the most productive countries and has a 35 hour week. Our contracted hours may say 35 to 40, but in many cases the reality is very different; 50 to 55 working hours is just not acceptable.

I Co-chair the National Forum for Health and Well-being at Work, which includes 25 companies and public sector bodies such as BT, BP, Shell, Rolls Royce, John Lewis Partnership, NHS England, the BBC, Microsoft, National College of Policing, UK government well-being lead, the Royal Mail, etc. They have highlighted managing the use of technology as the second-most important factor in well-being. In the workplace, we are not managing e-mails and the techno stress that results, impacting employee health and relationships outside work, as employees are now available on e-mail 24/7. Most companies have no guidelines at all, such as a policy that you only cc people who really need to be included in e-mails or only e-mail in working hours with managers avoiding sending e-mails outside of working hours to their staff unless absolutely necessary.

HR should be helping their organizations develop a well-being architecture specific to it, focusing on what are the most important issues for that organization and its employees.

In your experience what impact can performance management have on employee well-being (negative and positive) and what are your views on the performance appraisal and well-being?

My own view is that you need to have socially sensitive managers, and they should be doing performance 'appraisals' every day. I am 100 per cent against the annual appraisal because it is not happening at a specific time when an individual is performing really well or when performance is problematic. For well-being, feedback should be timely, both constructive feedback and praise. When feedback is timely it is easier to provide some specific examples to support the feedback. Where feedback lacks specific examples, the individual can feel confused and helpless, unable to take control of their performance moving forward.

What key things should an organization focus on in terms of performance management to support and enhance employee well-being?

There are a couple of key things. Firstly, when you performance manage, ensure it is not just critical. It is also about being positive. Praise! Then the organization needs to ensure that their line managers have the 'skill set' to do this. Organizations need to get more socially skilled people in management positions supported through training and development. Line managers need to understand the most effective way to performance manage people, to get the best out of them. How do we learn and grow without feedback? The best person to do that is usually your line manager. It is important to reinforce good performance with recognition. An American company found managers were not giving that recognition and put in place a short-term initiative where they could hand out a certain number of money-based vouchers to employees who performed above and beyond their job description to metaphorically say 'thank you for what you did'. It is important to embed 'recognition' into the organization culture.

For the reader who is keen to learn more about well-being in the workplace, where should they go to learn more?

Wellbeing: Productivity and Happiness at Work by Johnson, Robertson and Cooper (Palgrave Macmillan, 2018), which contains some great case studies of what organizations can achieve.

High-performance working

Over the last decade there has been much interest in the concept of 'high performance' or 'high-commitment' work organization and practices. The 2005 study by the Department of Trade and Industry (DTI) and the CIPD into high-performance work strategies identified a range of good practice 'high performance work practices' (HPWPs). Performance review, appraisal and career development formed key aspects of this good practice. Providing a forum for managers to communicate with their staff, and align individual performance to organizational goals, is seen to have a significant impact on areas such as customer satisfaction, quality of output and overall bottom-line performance. Performance management processes that encourage motivation and commitment, support learning and development, align people and processes to organizational objectives, and are managed fairly against a backdrop of trust can impact very positively on the overall performance of the organization.

Talent management

Talent management is about the identification, nurture, progress, reward and retention of key individuals who can aid the development of organizational sustainability' (Marchington and Wilkinson, 2012).

Back in 1998 the consultancy firm McKinsey introduced us to the concept of 'the war for talent', identifying talent management as a critical challenge for organizations. Since that time there has been a growth in interest in talent management, with a general recognition of the importance for organization success of attracting and retaining talent. Achievement of a competitive edge and sustainability in performance are seen as closely related to effective talent management. Globalization (requiring mobility of talent) and a more transitory perspective on careers, particular from younger workers, means that organizations need to think carefully about the management and development of employees' careers.

Whether you take the 'exclusive' view of talent management, focusing on a few key employees who have the potential to have a significant impact on the organization performance – or the 'inclusive' view, concerned with enabling all employees to maximize their potential – performance management, and in particular the performance review, has an integral role in delivering effective talent management. Whilst recruitment and selection has a key role in attracting talent into the organization and in creating talent pipelines, performance management has a key role in ensuring that talent is developed and retained in the organization.

Performance management processes when working effectively should help identify those employees with the potential and desire to grow and progress their careers within the organization, and provide essential data to feed into the career development, succession planning and reward management processes in the organization. Performance management should provide integration between these processes (integration is discussed in greater depth in Chapter 3). Given below is a case study demonstrating how Talent Management at Jumeirah Hotels is being used to drive the achievement of business goals.

CASE STUDY Harnessing talent and driving performance at Jumeirah Hotels

Jumeirah Hotels, Resorts and Residences are regarded as among the most luxurious and innovative in the world, winning numerous international awards. Founded in 1997, the luxury hotel group has a brand promise of 'Stay Different' to create 'imaginative and exhilarating experiences in culturally connected environments with thoughtful and generous hospitality'. The Burj Al Arab Jumeirah, their iconic property in Dubai, is a powerful symbol of this organization's success in delivering unique, luxurious experiences.

The business challenge and overall learning and development approach to building capability

Back in 2014 Jumeirah faced some key business challenges:

- Jumeirah's desire to double their portfolio size within 10 years – requiring a pipeline of talent (approximately 184 colleagues) at executive level.

- Hire to promotion ratio was 70:30 respectively. With recruiters charging 25 per cent of candidate salary and with data showing that 50 per cent of executives came through an agency, this could be very expensive – potentially £1.25m.

- There was a need to identify functional experts who were cultural ambassadors to be Pre-Opening Task Force Champions.

- A requirement to retain HoDs and particularly 'High Performing/High Potential Talent'. Turnover at executive level was near zero, limiting promotion opportunities. Therefore, engaging this cohort through investing in their development was vital.

- There was no L&D programme to develop HoDs to executive level.

The resulting L&D initiative sought to tackle these issues head on. The approach was to:

- Interview and partner with key senior leaders/project sponsors to determine what their 'end in mind' was. Coaching them to elicit objectives, desired performance behaviours and key areas to design into the development programme.
- Take advantage of unutilized functionality of the Talent Management System to document details of 'Talent'.
- Adapt the 'traditional 9 box' matrix approach, to include Flight Risk and Task Force Potential, supporting selection of the first cohort of learners.
- Create a pioneering, accelerated development programme; designed to develop high potential (HiPo) HoDs to executive level 12–18 months from completion.

The skills and capabilities that were the focal point for improvement: their importance and the challenges

The resulting 'HiPo' programme took a multifaceted, blended learning approach. It acknowledged 'learning' not being an 'event', but the timescale for new perspectives and behaviours being formed subjective to the individual. A literature review provided the insight that skill acquisition and talent growth could be accelerated through 'meaningful practice', feedback and immersion in stretching situations.

Senior leader interviews, capability gap analysis and research of 'best in class' interventions determined that the programme should focus on three key core areas. These were established as the most important areas of competence that Jumeirah's future leaders would require to leverage success.

- 'Leadership' – coaching and mentoring skills, project management and emotional intelligence.
- 'Commercial Acumen' – scanning the future business environment for opportunities and threats and developing a commercial strategy using the individual components of revenue, sales and marketing.
- 'Financial Awareness' – looking beyond financial statements to analysis, cash management, control frameworks and growing assets.

Each learner inevitably had different levels of competence and career aspirations; therefore, the programme included interventions that were more bespoke. An executive colleague skill audit was utilized to assist with this process.

Delivery of the initiative across the business and the results and measurement methodology

The HiPo initiative was delivered via a number of integrated interventions. Some examples are outlined below:

- rigorous selection process and targeted communications campaign;
- kick off webinar to outline the programme, timelines and expectations;
- webinar to mentors;
- international Pre-Opening Task Force opportunity;
- three-day business workshop;
- WhatsApp learner group – to drip feed articles, reminders, generate discussions and hold HiPos accountable;
- a mentor (two levels above the learner) matched according to key learning gaps;
- graduation presentation highlighting achievements and learning;
- hotel-based projects selected by general managers to impact the Hotels' KPIs;
- individual development plans.

Methods to measure and evaluate the programme were purposely integrated into the design, with a particular focus on the KirkPatrick models Level 3 (Behaviour Change) and Level 4 (Business Results).

The Level 3 results included:

- Post-programme skills audit identified an improvement in 89 per cent of target skills.
- Heightened confidence, improved leadership and coaching skills as validated by the delegates' teams and stakeholders.
- Common themes highlighted in feedback collated from the delegates' managers highlighted 'self/social awareness'; 'more open and engaging'; 'proactive approach to understating colleagues' needs' and greater 'adaptability'.
- Appraisal scores for the delegates increased on average by +0.7 (rating scale of 1–5).
- Increased innovation ideas including new sensory branding developed for one hotel.
- Through a modified process and empowerment, there has been a 60 per cent reduction in time to complete Finance Month End (from five days to two days), resulting in payroll and lieu time accumulation savings.

Embedding the learning and impact of the initiative for the business

The key to embedding the learning in the business was by making it a 'process', where learners were required to reflect (learning journals) and apply learning (new interventions and business scenarios/projects) and share with their direct reports and teams. The learning was also embedded by shifting the delegates' mindsets; realizing that the new concepts deliver very real results.

The key Level 4 results were:

- Fifty per cent of colleagues were promoted by completion of the programme – delivering a £40K recruitment costs saving (based on historical usage of recruiters).

- Guest satisfaction scores for the relevant operations departments that the colleague was leading increased on average by a huge 19.95 per cent YTD.

- Lead measures to colleague engagement indicated an increase, eg colleague turnover was down by 7 per cent.

- The HiPos enhanced leadership and competence contributed towards an increase in EBITDA across their operations, partly through maintaining food costs percentage at 26 per cent and reducing payroll.

These Level 4 results were achieved within 12–18 months after the programme started.

Jumeirah's High Potential (HiPo) programme was recognized by human resources professionals within the UK hospitality industry, receiving the award for 'Excellence in Learning & Development' at the HR in Hospitality's 2017 awards ceremony.

Conclusion

Performance management has attracted critics over the years, both from employees and managers in organizations, and from academics. Some of the major criticisms focus on the unnecessary bureaucracy that is seen to accompany many of its activities and the absence of any tangible positive outcomes at the end of many of the processes. There is, however, much evidence to show that when performance management is carried out well, in line with many of the themes that are explored in this book, there can be some clear benefits for organizations. Key benefits explored in this chapter have been:

- A greater ability to both manage and create change, with employees having the required skills, knowledge and confidence.

- Motivated employees who are more likely to deliver high levels of performance and demonstrate discretionary behaviour.

- Support for the maintenance of a healthy psychological contract, which research has demonstrated can lead to positive attitudinal and behavioural outcomes in employees – a key outcome being a decision to stay within an organization and a desire to contribute to that organization.

- A positive employer brand. This will impact both on the organization's ability to attract in top talent, positioning your organization as an employer of choice, but also on the ability to retain existing talent and minimize costs related to high turnover and recruitment and selection.

- Effective performance management systems help organizations to work within the framework of employment law and help ensure organizations manage their people ethically. Business ethics are an important issue for graduates entering employment in the 21st century, certainly compared to previous generations. It appears that ethical behaviour in business is a much more significant factor influencing the employment relationship – and organizations need to be aware of this when aiming to attract graduates into the company and, indeed, as part of their wider recruitment strategy.

- Performance management has an important part to play in the promotion of employee well-being in organizations. In turn there is growing evidence to demonstrate the positive impact of well-being on how individuals perform at work.

- Effective performance management has been shown to have the potential to impact very positively on overall organization performance, delivering high-performance working.

Indeed it is also helpful to reflect on some of the potential negative outcomes associated with an absence of effective performance management processes in an organization:

- poor levels of performance and responsiveness to change;

- demotivated, disengaged employees;

- breaches of the psychological contract, leading to low levels of trust and negative attitudinal and behavioural outcomes;

- negative employer brand, leading to challenges in recruiting new employees and retaining existing employees;

- high levels of staff turnover and absence;

- conflict in employee relations (rising levels of grievances, disciplinaries and possibly a growing incidence of employment tribunal cases being brought against the organization).

Action plan

Consider your responses to the seven statements outlined in Table 2.1. You may now find it helpful to start working on an action plan for performance management in your organization.

TABLE 2.1 Self-reflection questionnaire and action plan

On a scale of 1–5 where 1 is 'strongly disagree' and 5 is 'strongly agree', rate your current organization against the following statements (you may find it helpful to consider your own personal experiences here).

1 Performance management processes help the organization to manage and create necessary change.
  1 2 3 4 5

2 Performance management processes motivate employees to deliver high performance and demonstrate discretionary behaviour.
  1 2 3 4 5

3 Performance management processes help the organization sustain a healthy psychological contract.
  1 2 3 4 5

4 Performance management processes help maintain and develop a positive employer brand.
  1 2 3 4 5

5 Performance management processes help the organization operate legally and fairly.
  1 2 3 4 5

6 Performance management processes promote employee well-being.
  1 2 3 4 5

7 Performance management processes lead to clear, positive outcomes for my organization.
  1 2 3 4 5

Where you have responded positively, giving 4 and 5 ratings as your response, try to identify how performance management is delivering those positive outcomes. Is it a specific activity, or the way in which that activity is being implemented? These are the areas the organization needs 'to bottle'. Capture these good practices and aim to share and develop good practice across your organization. Quite often there are pockets of good practice within organizations, but opportunities to capture and share these good practices are missed.

Where you have responded negatively or neutrally to the statements, giving 1–3 ratings as your response, consider what the organization needs to start doing or do differently in terms of performance management in order to lead to more positive outcomes and added value. You may find it helpful to get other people in your organization to complete this short questionnaire – someone else within the HR team and maybe a senior manager outside of the HR department. Does their perspective agree with or differ from yours? Why do you think this is?

As you work through this book, you will identify more ways in which performance management can deliver positive outcomes for your organization. You may find it helpful to return to this action plan and develop further your ideas for improving practice in your organization.

How does it fit with organization and HRM strategy?

Strategic performance management

Defining a strategic approach

Before we examine strategic performance management it is worthwhile taking a more holistic look at the concept of strategy and strategic human resource management (HRM) in general. Over the years I have encountered some HR professionals who appear to visibly stiffen as soon as the word 'strategic' is mentioned. There often appears to be a sense that anything strategic is going to be either too difficult to understand or beyond the remit of the role of an HR professional who is working in any role below that of a director. Fortunately, this seems to be changing and the CIPD have championed the role of all HR professionals in delivering insight to support organizational goals.

It could be argued that the term 'human resource management' in itself implies 'strategic' without the prefix. Much of the debate around the change of terminology from 'personnel' to 'HRM' has focused on the issue of the strategic focus and proactive nature of HRM. Indeed I feel that Storey's (1995: 5) definition of HRM encapsulates the essence of strategic HRM as 'a distinctive approach to employment management which seeks to achieve competitive advantage through the strategic development of a highly committed and capable workforce, using an integrated array of cultural, structural and personnel techniques'. Strategic HRM can and should be understandable and relevant to all HR professionals. Once individuals get beyond their fear of some of the language used in relation to strategy, it can become more accessible for all. So let's start by breaking down some of the terminology, using the example of an advertising agency as a backdrop to our definitions:

- *Organization mission or vision statement*
  This is a general description of what the organization is for, its purpose, or its business: the reasons why this organization exists. It is usually succinct; in the case of an advertising agency it might be 'to produce superior advertising'.

- *Strategic goals*
  These are the intended results of pursuing the mission over a fixed time: in some cases long-term goals, in other short-term goals. For the advertising agency an example of a strategic goal might be 'to become the most profitable and highly creatively awarded advertising agency in London within the next five years'.

- *Strategic plan*
  This is the means through which the strategic goals are to be achieved. Decisions made here are vitally important. For the advertising agency it might be that the organization decides it needs to invest in the creative department, or focus on new business activity as there are significant concerns relating to current client spending plans. Strategic goals and plans at this level are often referred to as corporate strategy, the process for developing and defining a sense of direction. From the corporate strategy should flow functional or department strategic plans. With our agency example, investment in the creative department is likely to require an appropriate strategic response from the HR function, in terms of a recruitment and selection strategy to bring in top talent, but also a talent retention strategy for current high performers in the creative department.

This is a fairly simple overview and obviously strategic planning will involve much more depth of detail, but it is important and helpful to articulate in simple terms the direction an organization is going in. This will enable individuals at whatever level in the organization to understand the direction and focus of the organization and therefore be more likely to understand and deliver the required performance to support the organization in delivering against the strategy. Without a clearly articulated strategy, organizations and the individuals working for it will lack a sense of direction and purpose, and the establishment of relevant and coherent policies and activities within the organization will be that much harder to achieve.

Formulation of strategy and the strategic context

HR professionals should be able to contribute to the development of strategy in a variety of ways. They can contribute to the development of the strategic planning process (as outlined below), identify specific HR strategic objectives and provide HR input to the formulation of other strategic objectives. A great deal has been written about strategic management, much of that goes beyond the remit of this book; however, it is important to understand the 'classical' strategic management process that typically consists of the following stages:

- establishing a mission statement and key strategic goals for an organization;
- conducting an analysis of the external environment, looking at opportunities for growth and potential threats;
- analysis of the internal organization, looking at strengths, weaknesses, structure, systems, resources and capabilities;
- setting specific goals;
- examining options to achieve those goals;
- adopting plans to achieve goals;
- conducting regular reviews and evaluation of progress of plans against strategic goals.

Typical criticisms of this classical approach focus on the linear, top-down nature of this approach and emphasize the importance of also capturing information from the lower, grass-roots level of the organization and allowing that to be factored into the strategic process. Criticisms also focus on the lack of flexibility, and here perhaps the final bullet point of review and evaluation and continued analysis, both within and outside the organization, become extremely important. It may be that the best approach is to have strategies that combine a deliberate, analytical, controlling response with a responsiveness to change and ability to harness ongoing organizational learning.

PESTLE and SWOT

Organizations do not exist in a bubble, immune to the context in which they operate. Therefore, as identified in the 'classical' strategic management process examined at the start of this chapter, analysis of the external environment and organization context is a vital ingredient in strategic planning. Two techniques are helpful in this process, represented by the mnemonics PESTLE and SWOT:

- Political – how will political change at local, national or international level impact on this organization?

- Economic – what is the potential impact of economic indicators (for example, gross domestic product growth, inflation, interest or exchange rates)?

- Social – how will social trends impact on this organization (for example, consider the impact of social networking over the last couple of years)?

- Technological – how will developments in technology impact on how this organization operates in the future?

- Legal – what changes are expected and what impact are they likely to have on the organization?

- Environment – how might changes to the environment and changes to environmental practice affect the organization?

- Strengths – the valuable and successful aspects of the organization, such as a highly skilled and knowledgeable workforce.

- Weaknesses – the organization's negative features, such as poor employee relations.

- Opportunities – looking outside of the organization, what opportunities are there for the organization to take advantage of? For example, a competitor may be closing down and there may be an opportunity to bring some fresh talent into the organization.

- Threats – again looking outside of the organization, what developments may provide a threat or damage the organization's performance? For example, a competitor may be offering attractive compensation packages designed to attract your existing talent.

SWOT analysis provides an excellent framework to analyse the organization's current situation internally and externally. It is particularly helpful to try to marry up strengths with opportunities in your planning process. PESTLE considers current and future trends in the environment, which may impact on how the organization can and should function moving forward.

Activity

Draw up a PESTLE and SWOT for your organization. You may find it helpful just to focus on the current approach to performance management, rather than the entirety of HRM activity, but take whichever approach is most useful for you. For PESTLE, consider the environmental factors likely to impact on how your organization can and should performance manage its human resource over the next few years. You may find it helpful to talk to other members of the HR team and gain their views. For the SWOT analysis, complete the template provided in Table 3.1. Some questions have been added into the four zones to prompt your thinking, but they are not intended to be in any way comprehensive.

TABLE 3.1 A SWOT for your organization

STRENGTHS	WEAKNESSES
What do you do well?	What could you improve?
What resources and processes are valuable?	Where do you lack resources or have inefficient or ineffective processes?
OPPORTUNITIES	**THREATS**
What opportunities are available? What new trends or resources can you take advantage of?	What threats could impact on performance management?
	What are your competitors doing?
How can you turn your strengths into opportunities?	What threats do your weaknesses expose you to?

Approaches to strategic human resource management

One of the biggest criticisms of HR over many years has been the failure to understand and support business goals, with HR being seen as an overhead rather than a department that adds concrete value to an organization. To understand how performance management can add value and support the achievement of goals it is important to explore some of the approaches to strategic performance management. Strategic HRM should ensure there is a link between employees and the organization, and integrate HRM strategies and activities with the corporate strategies. There are a wide range of different views on the best approach to achieve this, many falling within the two perspectives of 'best fit' versus 'best practice'.

The best-practice approach is sometimes also referred to as the 'universalistic approach'. The argument here is that there is an ideal set of HR practices that when followed should always add value whatever the organizational context. An important factor here is that those practices interlink, they are a coherent group of activities that support and reinforce each other, creating a blended set of best practice. Horizontal integration of HRM practices (recruitment and selection, performance management, reward, learning and development) is important to ensure these practices can improve each other. There are a variety of viewpoints on what constitutes best practice, but some typical examples are:

- sophisticated selection and recruitment processes;
- sophisticated induction programmes;
- two-way communication processes to keep everyone fully informed;
- employment security and internal promotion;
- effective use of job design to ensure flexibility, commitment and motivation;
- extensive training, learning and development;
- reduction of status differentials/harmonization.

Many authors have criticized the best-practice approach, starting with the point that a lack of agreement on the nature of best practice is a problem in itself. Most criticisms focus on the argument that what works well in one organization may not work well in another, which has different goals, management style, structure and culture.

The best-fit approach is sometimes referred to as the 'contingency approach' and emphasizes the importance of ensuring HRM strategies are appropriate for the organization and the context in which the organization operates. Best fit identifies a link between HRM and the achievement of competitive advantage. There is no belief in universal solutions; rather a requirement for HRM policies and practices that 'fit' and are appropriate to the situation of a particular employer. What is appropriate for one organization cannot just be simply transferred to another with the presumption that the same positive results will ensue. Key variables to be considered are factors such as the size and structure of the organization, the culture, the business strategy and the labour markets in which the organization competes.

Life cycle models and competitive advantage models are often used in relation to the contingency approach, to demonstrate the link between business strategy and HR practices. Sisson and Storey (2000) have used the business life cycle to explain why HRM practices change or vary between organizations. They identify four stages of the business life cycle: start-up, growth, maturity and decline, and argue that at each stage the type and range of HRM policies and processes will be shaped by the internal and external influences affecting the organization. Let us take the example of the start-up organization. At this stage we are likely to see a commitment to entrepreneurialism and a high requirement for flexibility. In the early stages of an organization there is unlikely to be any significant emphasis on formalized policies apart from those with a legal requirement as a backdrop (health and safety, employment law). It may well be that cost control has to be high and therefore, in terms of financial reward may be focused on long-term incentives rather than short-term reward.

There are clear limitations in categorizing and generalizing in this way. For example, many start-ups may be borne from existing organizations rather than being a complete new business. Also organizations do not necessarily follow a linear path, but you see much more fluidity of movement between the stages. However, the business life cycle does provide a useful framework for making connections between HR policies and business requirements.

Activity

The business life cycle

- Start-up – early stages of business, flexibility of operation and response key to enable the organization to grow and develop. Strong commitment to entrepreneurialism.

- Growth – as the organization grows beyond a certain size, formal policies and procedures begin to emerge in order to ensure that it builds upon earlier success. Entrepreneurs who started up may resist formalization and may even decide to leave.

- Maturity – as markets begin to mature, and surpluses level out, the business has to take stock of its activities and shift priorities to cope with possibly flatter growth.

- Decline – the process of decline brings to a head many problems as the business struggles to survive.

If we take the example of recruitment and selection practices, at the start-up phase budgets are likely to be tight, so the organization will be lean and hiring only key employees required for growth who can add value. Expertise in specialist, non-core business areas is likely to be bought in when required on a contract basis, for example, a lawyer contracted to set up employment contracts. At the growth stage of the business life cycle, recruitment and selection is likely to be the lifeblood of the organization. A strong recruitment and selection strategy will need to be in place to ensure a strong flow of people into the organization with the skills, knowledge and attitude required. At the maturity stage there may be less expansion of headcount and, in order to manage labour costs, in some cases people leaving may not be replaced. At the decline phase much less recruitment and selection will be taking place apart from key positions such as those necessary for the survival of the organization. Thus the following questions need to be addressed:

- What stage of the business life cycle is your organization in?

- How does/should this influence the policies and practices of performance management?

- Can you identify another organization at a different stage of the business life cycle?

- How might their performance management policies and practices differ?

Another best-fit approach is to use competitive advantage models such as Porter's (1985) ideas on competitive strategy to HRM. This is an alternative method of 'matching' HR strategies to the corporate strategy of the organization. Porter (1985) argued that employers generally have three strategic options: to compete on cost, to compete on quality or to compete through innovation.

- *HR and cost reduction*

  Here the focus will be on minimizing costs. It may be that some HR activities are outsourced to improve cost-effectiveness. Learning and development (L&D) investment may be limited to essential skill and health and safety requirements. There is likely to be little in the way of employee involvement activity. Performance management practices will focus on the 'exchange' employment relationship; communicating requirements and identifying reward for delivering performance. This simplistic approach has echoes of Taylorism, with the use of short-term goals and a results-orientated focus.

- *HR and quality*

  Here you are likely to see a well-resourced, proactive HR function, driving best-practice activity across the organization. There is a much more sophisticated approach to performance management than in the cost-reduction organization; focused on how employees perform as well as the outputs. There is likely to be high levels of employee participation in decisions relating to the job and immediate work environment. It is likely that the use of competencies will be in evidence both in recruitment and selection and performance management, and a significant investment in learning and development to support the delivery of high performance.

- *HR and innovation*

  It may be a strategy for the entire organization, but it is likely that there will be specific departments or units focused on competing through innovation. Where there is a focus on a strategy of innovation you are likely to see an emphasis on informality, problem solving and creativity. Here we need to be as far from the 'controlling' side of performance management as possible. There will need to be a greater tolerance of risk-taking and ambiguity. Creativity requires space, so more loosely worded objectives and longer-term goals, with incentive rewards for innovation likely to be in evidence here.

I have found when asking HR professionals which of these approaches (best fit versus best practice) they find most relevant or appropriate, that the response has been overwhelmingly 'best fit'. However, interestingly when I have asked which approach is most evident in their own organizations, the response is more evenly shared between the two approaches. I believe that there are many circumstances in which a best-practice approach may be appropriately employed by an organization:

- When there is lack of a clearly communicated corporate strategy with which to align HR strategies.

- For organizations at the start-up phase of business where the nature of the organization is still being shaped.

- For organizations experiencing significant ongoing change. In these circumstances it may be safer to follow best practice than align to a strategy/culture that is in a state of flux.

- Because it is sometimes easier! Vertical alignment requires access to corporate strategy and, ideally, for the HR function to be given a strategic place in the organization, which may be hard to achieve in some organizations.

I have found that many organizations will first identify best practice through looking at other organizations' practices and established guidance from bodies such as the CIPD, but will then shape those practices to fit their own particular circumstances and strategic and operational requirements. Indeed, over the last few years there has been a degree of push back on the use of the term 'best practice'. Many HR practitioners that I have taught and work with now prefer to use the term 'good practice'. This would imply that in many situations there is a range of good practices that might be appropriate and add value and others that might not. Using their organizational insight, the HR practitioner should be able to advise on those good practices appropriate to meet existing and future needs.

A third approach is referred to as the configuration approach or 'bundling'. Some argue that this presents a middle-ground or halfway house between the best-practice and best-fit approaches discussed above. There is an emphasis here both on vertical alignment and horizontal fit. Bundles of HR practices that interrelate, reinforce and support each other are identified in order to contribute to the achievement of the organization's strategies. The emphasis here is on a holistic approach; not a piecemeal series of HR interventions, but a coherent, unified approach. There is limited agreement on the exact combination of HR practices, as any bundles suggested by researchers tend to be industry-specific. However, there does appear to be considerable agreement that HR practices are more likely to be effective when they work in combination. For example, the introduction of self-managing teams will require a significant investment in learning and development.

An alternative approach is to adopt the resource-based view, which is based on the premise that to achieve competitive advantage you need to attract and retain people who are better than those employed by your competitors. The focus here is on the development of human capital for sustained competitive advantage. The resource-based approach is interesting because it takes a bottom-up rather than top-down approach, focusing on existing resource rather than the particular strategy of the organization. Effective analysis of what is required in terms of HR is supported by sophisticated recruitment and selection and a performance management system that harnesses the strengths of an organization's human resource and supports development with a strong focus on learning and development. Performance management should provide both financial and non-financial reward (see below) to recognize valuable skills and behaviours. Skills, knowledge, attitudes and competencies are all important and should be evident through the performance management processes. Criticisms of this approach are that it fails to pay enough attention to the external context and competitive strategies.

An integrated approach

Strategic performance management

The themes of horizontal and vertical integration are clearly important in any discussion about strategic HRM practices. It could be argued that nowhere do they have greater importance than in the area of performance management, which relies on the effective integration of a wide range of HR activities, including but not exclusively, recruitment and selection, induction, learning and development and reward management. So how do you achieve integration in practice? Integration appears to be more straightforward where there is an integrated HR function within a fairly simple organization structure. Where HR operates in separate silos, within a more complex structure, integration can be more of a challenge. The key here is strong communication between the different areas of HRM, from the planning stage through to execution and evaluation of all HR activities.

Performance management and recruitment and selection

Performance management commences with the recruitment and selection process. Job analysis – which forms part of the recruitment process – should form the basis of the performance agreement when chosen candidates commence employment with the organization (see Chapter 6). It is really important that organization values and core competencies identified at the heart of performance management are integrated into the recruitment and selection process. From the point that a candidate accesses data about a vacant position they are forming an understanding of what the organization expects in terms of performance – and it is vital that there is a clear connection between that early communication with a potential candidate and the reality of working for the organization. During the selection process, candidates must be given an accurate picture of performance expectations, so all employees involved in the selection process must share a consistent understanding of the requirement of the job.

Likewise the selection tools chosen must be designed to assess the skills and behaviours required for the role. A person I worked with several years ago told me about their experience of applying for a junior accountancy role. As part of the selection process they were given a series of tests, for which the instructions were written in such a complex way that what was actually being tested was a high level of English language capability rather than the mathematical skill required for the job. Selection tools such as this are not only unfair, but give candidates a false impression of the skills and knowledge required to carry out the job, so even if they perform well in the test they might choose to deselect from the process.

During the recruitment and selection process, if done well, there should be a rich source of accurate data about a candidate's past performance, experience, skills and competency set and also performance potential. Unfortunately in some cases, once this rich data has been collected and the selection process is completed, this information can then sit gathering 'dust' on an individual's personnel file, possibly until the file is discarded some time after they leave the organization. With most records being held electronically these days, there is no excuse for not enabling this data to flow into performance management systems. The data on experience, skills, competencies and performance potential may not all be relevant to the current role the individual is being selected for, but may offer valuable data for personal development plans. It is particularly useful in matrix- or project-based organizations, where experience with certain clients may not be immediately useful but when a new account is won or is to be pitched for this data may be invaluable in putting a team together.

Recent resourcing and talent planning surveys conducted by the CIPD have revealed that despite a tough economic climate over the last few years, organizations are still having difficulty selecting candidates who meet all their essential, let alone desirable, criteria in the person specifications. There are still shortages of candidates with the right skills and knowledge for jobs. Because of this one of the key strategies used by many organizations is to hire people who may not meet all requirements and then develop those skills/ knowledge once the individual has joined the organization. Any shortfall in meeting performance criteria must therefore be fed into the performance management process so that the addressing of this shortfall can be resourced adequately by an appropriate intervention (for example, coaching by a line manager, a training course or provision of a mentor).

Usually the person managing a new recruit has been involved in the selection process, but this is not always the case and it is really important that they are made aware of any shortfall in meeting the performance criteria so that they can support the individual in reaching the required standards. I have heard of situations where a manager disappointed early on with a new recruit's performance has then responded negatively to the individual, when clearly the underperformance at this point is not their fault. The expectations that a line manager should have of a new recruit should be clearly communicated from the team involved in the recruitment and selection process, and a plan put in place to enable the individual to develop the required skills or knowledge that they lack at the point of recruitment.

Induction

A key element in the integration of performance management with recruitment and selection is the induction process. The two-way exchange of information during this process should facilitate the integration process. The way that new recruits are inducted into an organization has a direct impact on their ability to reach the desired performance requirements as quickly as possible. An effective induction process will enable new recruits to become productive quickly, by delivering the following:

- Clear communication of performance expectations (which should be reinforcing what has been communicated during the recruitment and selection process). Performance expectations will cover not only 'what' needs to be done, but the 'how' of performance – the required behaviours.

- Clear communication of the 'rules of the game'. By this I mean an outline of what is expected in terms of behaviour, but also what is unacceptable behaviour. Company handbooks will have a core role in this, but it is very important for any future management of underperformance that behavioural expectations have been clearly outlined at the start of employment and that there is evidence that this has taken place.

- Creating an environment where an employee is motivated to perform. Early days in the job have a strong impact on whether the individual feels enthused by his or her job choice or demotivated, feeling he or she has made the wrong decision: this is sometimes referred to as 'the induction crisis'. Motivation theory has been discussed earlier, in Chapter 2, but those theories that emphasize the communication of clear, stretching goals, timely and regular feedback on performance and a sense of fairness and being valued are all key factors to be considered and delivered through the induction experience.

- Socialization – research has shown that socialization is as important as effective selection in ensuring a recruit delivers against performance expectations and feels motivated to perform against those expectations. Socialization enables new recruits to develop work relationships through formal interventions such as team-building events but also more informal socializing.

Too often induction is seen by managers as an annoyance that interrupts operation needs, and once the one- or two-day training with HR is completed there is a sense of relief that 'that box is ticked'. There is a tricky balance to be achieved between operation needs and the need to deliver the required information. Ideally a tailored approach will be taken, recognizing the needs of the stakeholders, rather than a simplistic 'sheep dip' approach. However, such an approach is not always practical or affordable. Induction should, however, be recognized as a process rather than a one-off event and needs to be owned by all the stakeholders who have an interest in an employee's performance. With such an approach, gradually as the employee begins to feel part of the organization and starts to deliver the performance required, there is a natural flow from induction into the ongoing performance management process.

CASE STUDY   Socialization and induction

One London-based media company had an interesting approach to the socialization process. HR would organize regular new-starter lunches that would be attended by a member of the senior management team. The seniority and role of the new starter was irrelevant: everyone who had joined over a recent period would come together for sandwiches, an informal presentation by a senior member of management and to learn more about the culture of the organization and other members of staff who had recently joined the organization. The senior member of staff would talk about their experience of working for the company, the things they enjoyed, the opportunities, but also some of the challenges. New recruits were encouraged to talk about their role and why they had joined the company, and share what had attracted them to the organization. The company identified several key benefits to emerge from these lunches:

- Improvement of communication between staff and the senior management team. The team were felt to be more accessible as most members of staff felt that there was someone in the team they would feel comfortable in approaching if they needed to.

- Improved communication between different functional areas in the organization. Quite often employees can commence work in a particular area and then, unless their job requires it, have little contact with other parts of the organization. Meeting people from other departments early on and finding out about their roles really helped people get a sense of the wider organization they were a part of. Lunches also provided employees with a contact in other departments who they could approach when needed. This was particularly valued by some of the more junior members or less confident members of staff. Their initial contact might not be the person they needed, but it gave them a starting point of contact.

- Motivation and commitment – these lunches celebrated the culture and successes of the organization and highlighted the positive reasons why people had joined. Feedback from new recruits after these lunches mostly confirmed that they found them a motivating experience and felt committed to their new roles.

Performance management and reward

Whilst there is an ongoing debate over the issue of whether performance management should have a developmental focus, or be focused on integration with pay, there is little debate over the need for a consistent and coherent approach to people management in terms of performance management and reward strategy and processes. Some organizations cling to their 'service' reward culture, which provides benefits and rewards linked to the length of service with the company, and then wonder why turnover amongst new recruits is high. In terms of the question, 'What should the company reward?' – my simple response is that the company should reward what is valuable to the organization. What behaviours, what output, what values will drive the organization towards achievement of its goals? Recognize those things in your people and then reward them. For example, many HR departments struggle to get managers to prioritize people management issues, such as completion of appraisals or personal development plans, against a backdrop of other core operational demands. Unless these managers feel that their performance in the area of people management will be reviewed by the company – is seen as valuable to the company and will be recognized by the company – they may well choose to place it at the bottom of their list of priorities.

One organization I worked with was struggling to get regional managing directors to focus on people management issues. They decided to implement a company-wide employee engagement survey. The results of this survey, alongside other operation results areas, were then directly linked to the regional managing directors' annual bonuses. Not surprisingly, performance in the area of people management moved fairly swiftly higher up the MDs' list of priorities!

Total reward

When discussing the integration of reward and performance management, it is important to emphasize that we are talking about the concept of total reward. This concept brings together all types of reward – financial and non-financial – as an integrated and coherent whole. A consistent message in relation to what the organization values should flow out of the different types of reward and should reinforce the message communicated through the performance objectives outlined in the performance management process: 'A total reward approach is holistic, reliance is not placed on one or two reward mechanisms operating in isolation, account is taken of every way in which people can be rewarded and obtain satisfaction through their work' (Armstrong and Baron, 2005: 103). Wilton (2011: 217) provides an excellent summation of the need for integration: 'Reward constitutes a principal means by which employers attempt to generate and direct required effort and behaviours to be consistent with organization objectives. It is important... that employers are mindful of the signal transmitted by their reward strategy, systems and practices and ensure that the connection between reward and behaviour are effectively communicated.' If there is a disconnect between the signal transmitted from reward strategy and that of performance management, the organization is unlikely to achieve the type of performance it requires to achieve organizational goals.

Examples of non-financial reward are as follows:

- recognition;
- opportunities to develop skills and knowledge;
- career opportunities;
- quality of working life, such as flexible working practices.

Herzberg (1968) would argue that these are the true elements at work that motivate, and that financial reward is merely a hygiene factor that causes dissatisfaction when we are not happy with 'the deal'. More recent research by Daniel Pink (2011) reinforces the limitations of financial reward on employee motivation. He suggests that organizations should ensure that the issue of money is 'taken off the table' by paying people sufficiently/fairly for work provided, and that then organizations should focus on providing opportunities for people to have autonomy and mastery at work in order to create a motivating working environment. Research conducted with know-ledge workers tends to show that financial reward is not the most valued element in the total reward package.

Effective performance management will identify an individual's motivators and, if possible (and where realistic for the organization), will aim to provide an environment that provides those motivators. Understanding what motivates an individual is clearly a vital element of recruitment and selection, but performance management needs to ensure that this understanding continues throughout employment. Not only are employees motivated by different things, but motivators can change over time. For example, whilst there are some similarities in terms of motivators for me now as compared to me the young graduate entering the job market for the first time, there are also some significant differences. Performance management can facilitate a dialogue through which an understanding of an individual's motivators can be maintained. The line manager can have a strong impact on the positive delivery of non-financial rewards.

Financial reward

In some organizations the main purpose of performance management is to generate data from which decisions are then made regarding pay reviews or bonuses. There continues to be considerable debate about the challenge of combining a clear link with reward in performance management with a developmental approach. This may be particularly problematic when ratings are used, and individuals may be reluctant to admit areas for development/

improvement when at the front of their mind is the achievement of a rating link to financial reward. Whilst there may be some benefit in holding a pay review or bonus discussion away from a performance appraisal, the fact remains that a fair, transparent reward system is reliant on an accurate assessment of performance in the job (a full discussion of ratings can be found in Chapter 7).

There is also continued debate around the concept of money as a motivator. There may be a natural tendency to critique the simplicity of Taylorism, but we shouldn't lose sight that for many people at work, their basic reason for being there – their motivation to turn up and deliver the work required – is to earn money. Individuals need to understand the nature of 'the deal', what is required in terms of performance and what reward will result if that performance is delivered. This should be communicated on commencement of employment and throughout employment, particularly when the nature of 'the deal' needs to change. This is very much about a contractual transaction. If, however, we wish our employees to go beyond contract, or offer some discretionary behaviour, then we may well be looking at factors beyond the basic financial exchange.

Some organizations choose to use some form of contingent pay: performance, competency or contribution-related pay for example, to motivate individuals to achieve specific targets or demonstrate certain behaviours or skills. Again, there is much debate about the validity of using such methods as motivators. Some argue that whilst a pay rise or a bonus may have a short-term impact on motivation levels, as time passes the impact on motivation will fade. Linking back to Vroom's expectancy theory discussed in the previous chapter, it is very important that where contingent pay is used, the employee believes that with a reasonable amount of effort the goal set is achievable. The employee needs to have a sense of control, a belief that he or she can have an impact on the end result. Vroom also tells us that the reward (financial or not) must be seen as valuable to the employee. Therefore, getting the reward strategy right to drive effective performance is extremely important for organizations.

I would argue that the link between performance management and financial reward is important, particularly in the context of equity, fairness and transparency, but so is the link with non-financial rewards. Indeed in the financial climate in recent years, where many pay increases/bonuses may be limited, or indeed packages frozen, organizations need to maximize use of non-financial rewards to recognize performance and demonstrate to employees that they are valued by the organization. A total reward strategy that is integrated with the performance management process is what is required.

The impact on the employer brand

The importance of a positive employer brand has been discussed in the previous chapter, but it is worth revisiting here in the context of the need for integration of HR processes. Over recent times there has been much well-documented controversy over senior management bonuses, particularly in industries such as banking. The controversy has highlighted a strong public belief that there should be a transparent link between performance and pay. Indeed, it is not only the employer brand, but the overall corporate brand that can be seriously damaged when the link between reward and performance is seen by the public to be weak, or unjust. To maintain a positive brand, and the respect and trust of those both within and outside of the organization, the integration between financial reward and performance delivered needs to be strong and needs to be transparent. Transparency can be reinforced through review of pay through joint consultative committees, works councils, governors and other elected representatives.

Performance management and learning and development

Performance management is about growth and improving performance. It is about raising the performance of individuals and teams to reach organizational goals and the achievement of ongoing improvement in performance levels. It is therefore vital that learning and development (L&D) activity in organizations is fully integrated with the performance management process. There are two main strands to achieving integration.

First, the rather mechanistic process of ensuring that any L&D needs identified during the process of objective setting – be they at organization, team or individual level – are resourced effectively and efficiently. This requires a robust communication process that is often, but not necessarily, supported by an HR database. It is very demotivating for an employee to be set objectives requiring L&D support only to find that that support is not forthcoming. Sometimes the budget isn't there for a particular learning intervention, but when this happens it should be explained to the individual and discussed with the line manager. It may well be that an alternative intervention can be identified that has lower cost implications. If support has not been forthcoming this needs to be taken into account in any future assessment of performance.

Second, integration can be supported by ensuring that performance management processes themselves create an environment where L&D can flourish. This is explored further in Chapter 6; however, it is worth highlighting here some of the factors that can support this:

- culture of regular feedback (praise and constructive criticism);
- incorporating L&D opportunities within the performance agreement;
- effective personal development planning;
- coaching or mentoring.

Many organizations today now recognize that learning isn't just about sending someone on a training course; rather it is important to maximize opportunities for learning and growth for employees as they carry out their roles.

Many organizations have adopted the 70:20:10 approach to learning. This suggests that 70 per cent of learning should come through experience and 20 per cent through social interaction, for example with work colleagues. That leaves the remaining 10 per cent of learning to be met by formal learning such as classroom or, increasingly, online courses. Whilst never intended to be a prescriptive formula I think 70:20:10 does highlight how important learning on the job is. Performance management has a significant role here in maximizing opportunities for learning. I would highlight two particular areas where performance management impacts here. First, the role of ongoing feedback both when someone is not performing in the most effective way and also when they are performing well. Feedback here will support the individual in learning what types of behaviour are required from the role and will support the delivery of superior performance. Second, in creating the space for reflection. As Kolb (1985) highlights, reflection is an important stage in learning and good line managers will create timely opportunities for individuals to reflect on their performance, both good and bad, and take learning from that reflection to improve or develop performance moving forward. Line management capability once again is a critical success factor here. Investing in more formal learning for these employees so they have strong skills in giving feedback and supporting reflection will reap rewards by creating an environment where opportunities to learn on the job are maximized.

The organization

Type and structure

In terms of 'fit' with the organization, performance management processes need to take into consideration the company's type and structure. Whether it is private sector, public sector or third sector (not-for-profit), the size and complexity of the organization and the structure (matrix, functional, divisional) should all be considered when adopting a performance management process. The type of organization will clearly impact on the company's goals and the identification of what effective performance looks like. Finding a performance management system that meets the needs of all areas of a large, complex organization may be challenging and not always viable. In some cases, performance management will need to be adapted to meet the requirements of different areas of the organization. As long as the core philosophy remains the same, however, flexibility in approach need not lead to inconsistency or confusion. For example, matrix organizations can present a particular challenge for performance management, with multi-reporting lines that may involve fairly short-term working relationships.

As well as driving the performance that the organization requires, performance management processes need to be practical for the circumstances of the organization. One of my past students worked for a Christian organization involved in managing a training facility. She identified that some approaches to managing performance, as recommended by her fellow students, would sit uncomfortably within the particular context of her organization. She had to spend considerable time thinking how best to employ good HR practice, but at the same time meet the particular needs of her organization. This supports the best-fit approach discussed earlier.

The flexible firm and the gig economy

As we move further into the 21st century, increasingly the traditional concept of work and working lives is being challenged. At the turn of the century Handy (2002) wrote about the 'shamrock organization, made up of the three segments of core workers, a flexible labour force and contractual fringe. It is that contractual fringe where we have seen a real growth in recent times. The term 'gig economy' has come into current parlance where work is contracted on a freelance short-term basis and often utilizes technology to connect workers and hirers. Sometimes now referred to as your 'agile talent', a traditional mindset in terms of managing performance may be problematic. For example, there is likely to be a greater need here for the worker to take real ownership over their own performance. However, that doesn't mean that organizations should neglect their agile workforce in terms of performance management (though many seem to be doing just that). Ensuring that these workers understand how their role aligns to the organization objectives, clarity in terms of what performance is required, feedback on performance, two-way communication and understanding the link between performance and reward (supporting motivation) are all performance management ingredients that are important in getting the best out of your agile workforce. However, HR and line managers may need to rethink how these are delivered. This is a challenge for all areas of HR, not just performance management, and as I write this is a fast-growing challenge for the profession and one where solutions are evolving.

With many organizations now working with a range of different working arrangements/employment relationships, a homogenized approach in terms of performance management many not always be realistic or appropriate.

Working across international boundaries

Particular challenges may be faced when implementing performance management in organizations that work across international boundaries. The particular challenges I have identified relate to the cultural differences that may exist between organizations. For example, in Western Europe people are mostly comfortable with providing upward feedback to someone in a more senior position in the organization; however, in many Asian countries where much more deference is exhibited to those in senior positions, employees may feel uncomfortable with this. Eastern European countries have taken some time to embrace the assessment of performance based on results and the use of performance management as a motivational tool, because in the communist era promotion was often related to loyalty and political status. Running roughshod over these cultural differences can do much damage, so it is important to do your research and identify strategies to manage these cultural differences, including providing training and support for those involved.

Organizations that adopt practices that consider the societal cultures they operate within can evidence impact in terms of reduction in staff turnover and lower levels of absenteeism. However, we are also seeing that as countries grow in economic maturity and the impact of globalization grows, there appears to be more opportunity for standardization of performance management practice. As ever, strong insight into your organization and the context in which it operates is key here.

Culture

It is also very important for performance management to fit the culture of the organization or, during a period of cultural change, support the shift to a new working culture. The culture of an organization can have a strong influence

on what people do at work and what they want to do (their
So what do we mean by culture? The intangible nature of c
it a challenge to define but the CIPD definition (2005) is help
of shared values and beliefs about what is important, what be
appropriate and about feelings and relationships internally an
Values and cultures need to be unique to the organization, widely shared and
reflected in daily practice and relevant to the company purpose and strategy.
But there is no single best culture.' Culture is also often referred to simply
as 'the way we do things round here'. Whilst a company handbook should
outline the rules and regulations under which the employment relationship is
carried out, the culture of the organization provides an informal framework
of behavioural norms. Usually the culture of the organization is led by the
senior management team, who 'model' behaviours that are then cascaded
down through the organization, with more junior members of staff aiming
to emulate their behaviours in order to progress within the organization.

The culture of an organization has a powerful impact on how people
behave, and if there is a disconnect between the culture of the organization
and the behaviours an organization's performance management processes
are aiming to encourage, the process will struggle to achieve its goals. For
example, consider an organization wishing to encourage and embed core
competencies such as 'innovation' and 'courage to challenge' through the
performance management process. If the current organization culture is
a bureaucratic one, with a strong focus on rules and procedures and an
emphasis on consistency and low risk-taking, the performance management
process will struggle to deliver. There is a disconnect here between the goals
of performance management and the existing culture of the organization.
Senior managers will have a key role here in starting to role-model new
behaviours if these new behaviours stand any chance of bedding in to the
organization.

The culture of the organization also needs to be carefully considered
when deciding on what type of performance management process is appropriate. For example, 360-degree feedback will struggle against a backdrop
of a 'blame culture' where there is low trust (see Chapter 6). Performance
management will be most successful when it reflects the core values of the
organization as demonstrated by the senior management team.

Management style

Closely aligned with the concept of culture is the prevalent management style.
The management style of the senior management team will have a strong impact
throughout the organization and will impact on performance management,

ᴗfluencing the type of processes that can work. For example, a performance management process that emphasizes upward feedback and a joint problem-solving approach may struggle in an organization where the prevalent management style is highly autocratic. Transactional and transformational styles (as highlighted in Chapter 1) can also have a strong impact on the approach taken to managing performance. Charismatic leadership may work particularly well with a performance management system that is achievement-focused, encourages calculated risk-taking and open communication.

Are your managers 'enablers', creating an environment where people can take on responsibility, autonomy and challenge – or are they 'controllers' who aim to ensure compliance and provide strong direction? If the organization is set on a particular path for performance management, it may be that there should be an honest appraisal of management style first – then, where there is a disconnect, put in place some supporting development to achieve behavioural change. There is some debate about how easy it is for managers to 'flex' their style, and in some cases organizations choose to make changes within the senior management team in order to create the cultural change to deliver effective performance.

So to conclude, performance management takes place within a context. There is the organization itself, its mission and strategic goals, the type of organization, and the organization's values and culture. There is also the external environment: for example, the economic backdrop and employment marketplace. It is important that performance management, if it is to deliver any value, is planned and executed taking the context into consideration. This chapter should help you to identify mechanisms that help the process of performance management in your organization add value. Here is a great example of strategic performance management in action at Hilton.

CASE STUDY Performance management at Hilton

At Hilton, our mission is simple: to be the most hospitable company in the world. Providing exceptional experiences to our guests is our top priority, and our team members are key to our success. It's therefore crucial that we provide meaningful opportunities that support and help them to excel in their careers. Rated a top 10 employer in the global Great Place to Work rankings and fifth in Europe, we're proud to have been recognized for our achievements in this space already, and constantly strive to improve where we can.

Performance management plays a central role in supporting team members, providing a platform to establish clear objectives and parameters for success with their line managers, so they can grow and thrive alongside our business.

For over eight years, we've been using a single accessible platform for performance management, compensation, talent reviews and learning, which helps ensure consistency and simplicity. It also enables senior leaders to analyse performance data to inform decisions about learning and development opportunities, rewards and recognition.

There are several important elements to our performance management process:

1 Objective and goal setting

Critical to supporting team members in their progression is the process of setting goals at the beginning of each year. Every team member, together with their manager, agrees on their objectives for the next 12 months and the competencies required to achieve these goals. Agreed goals and objectives are documented in the online platform, along with career development plans, and are referred to as progress is tracked throughout the year.

2 Frequent coaching and evaluation

As part of our developing performance management model, we encourage managers to share informal feedback throughout the year. We strongly believe that more emphasis should be put on these regular coaching sessions than the end-of-year review meeting because frequent check-ins can be hugely beneficial for team members' performance, progress, development and levels of engagement.

In a constantly changing environment, flexibility is also crucial. As part of these catch-ups, we stress that the relevance of predefined objectives should be reviewed and they should be amended if business needs change.

Finally, all team members are also regularly assessed against the same six core competencies, in line with the Hilton Values: hospitality, integrity, leadership, teamwork, ownership, now.

3 Annual review and reward

At the end of each year, more formal feedback is gathered by the manager using the online platform. This information provides a much richer assessment of the overall performance of the team member at the end of the period and helps to define the objectives for the subsequent year.

As a pay-for-performance organization, team member performance is rated during the end-of-year review and assessment. These ratings are used to inform compensation decisions for salary/merit increase, bonus payout and long-term incentive grant amounts.

4   *Training for managers*

We believe it's essential to provide custom coaching for managers so they feel confident in their ability to support their charges. Our leadership programmes help managers to learn how to have frequent, effective and honest conversations with their team members, and additional tools and resources are also available in our Hilton Performance Management Resource Centre.

As we continue to build our developing performance management system, we are committed to providing even more support to managers and team members so they feel confident engaging in more frequent dialogue and continuous feedback.

Alongside our formal performance management process, regular rewards through our benefits and learning opportunities are fundamental to keeping team members motivated. That's why we recently revealed new team member benefits such as industry-leading parental leave and adoption assistance, as well as boosted travel perks. Alongside these, Hilton University provides more than 5,000,000 hours of training each year through over 2,500 courses, delivered in a variety of training formats, including classroom training, e-learning, webinars, e-books, live and taped programmes, on-the-job and social learning experiences.

In a bid to increase team member resilience, focus and optimism about their work, we also recently launched Thrive@Hilton, a bespoke programme developed in partnership with experts at Thrive Global. Through initiatives such as building in time to recharge and daydream during the workday, sabbaticals and modern tools for time management, Thrive@Hilton will enable our team members to grow and flourish in body, mind and spirit.

ABOUT HILTON: Founded in 1919, Hilton (NYSE: HLT) is a leading global hospitality company, with a portfolio of 14 world-class brands comprising more than 5,100 properties with nearly 838,000 rooms in 103 countries and territories.

REFLECTION AND DIAGNOSTIC QUESTIONNAIRE

Managing performance should be a strategic activity. It should support the goals of the organization and fit the context of the organization. Think about the type of organization you work for. For example, is it private, public or third sector? What size is the organization and how is it structured (large, medium, small; functional, divisional, matrix)? How would you describe the culture of your organization? When you have identified this information start thinking about how this data might impact on how performance can/should be managed in your organization based on the context.

Reflect now on your organization's approach to performance management in terms of alignment and integration. Consider the questions set out in Table 3.2.

TABLE 3.2 Performance management in your organization: alignment and integration

1	How well does performance management link to the overall mission and values of the organization? Identify an example to demonstrate that link.
2	Do objectives set at an individual- or team-level link to the wider goals of the organization? Identify specific examples to show where there are links.

(continued)

TABLE 3.2   *(Continued)*

3	Is there a follow-through from recruitment and selection into the performance management process? Note down examples to show the link between these activities. What role does induction have in this?
4	What happens to data relating to learning and development needs captured in the performance management process? What links can you identify between performance management and learning and development?
5	Based on your responses to the questions above, assess how well performance management 'fits' your organization and demonstrates vertical alignment and horizontal integration.
6	How do you think performance management can achieve improved alignment and integration moving forwards?

This chapter has considered why and how performance management need. to achieve 'fit' with the organization and the strategic backdrop. Alignment and integration are two key factors in ensuring that performance management supports the unique circumstances of an organization. Alignment to the mission, values and goals of the organization, and integration with other areas of HRM activity, ensure that these areas of HRM are mutually reinforcing and driving forward the overarching HRM strategy effectively. In the next chapter we move away from the big picture of the organizational context to take a look at some of the operational areas of performance management in order to gain an understanding of how performance management works in practice.

How does it work?

As explored in the previous chapter, it is important that performance management is carried out giving careful thought to the organizational and business context. However, it is also true that certain basic principles and elements of good practice can be fairly consistently applied to many organizational situations and lead to positive outcomes. This chapter explores some of the activities, processes and behaviours most often identified as representing good practice, both in managing performance and conducting a performance review. One such area of good practice is that of the performance management cycle.

The performance management cycle

One criticism of performance management is that it is often carried out as a rigid top-down activity rather than as a flexible, continuous process that constantly evolves. Yet the concept of the performance management cycle fits well with the need for such an ongoing, continuous and evolutionary process: it should not be looked at as a once-a-year appraisal discussion, but instead should be seen as an ongoing process or cycle.

There are many perspectives on the nature of this cycle, but typically the stages will include the core activities of planning, action, monitoring and reviewing performance. The planning stage commences with the cascading down of corporate objectives to a team and individual level, with the aim of achieving vertical alignment. Performance criteria are then agreed between managers and individuals and then action plans are formulated to drive performance moving forward. As individuals carry out their jobs, their performance needs to be monitored on an ongoing basis to assess how well they are meeting the performance criteria. Monitoring is important for effective data capture (as discussed in Chapter 7). Performance should be monitored and feedback given to the individual on a regular basis, not waiting until a formal review of performance. Feedback enables the

FIGURE 4.1 The four stages of the performance management cycle

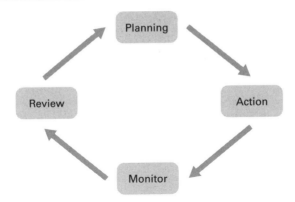

individual and the manager to assess whether actual performance is matching desired performance. Reviewing performance will enable the employee and manager to identify any performance gaps or development needs and take any required action.

The four stages of the performance management cycle – planning, action, monitoring and reviewing – are explored in more detail below, together with some of the key activities that are likely to be taking place at each stage and the role of the employee and the manager at each stage (see Figure 4.1).

Stage 1 – planning

Performance planning should align to the overall objectives of the organization and be developed within the context of the job description or role profile. Specific individual objectives and performance targets are defined, shared and agreed and time frames for achievement are outlined. A shared view of performance is very important as expectations must be clearly understood by the manager, the employee and any other stakeholders involved. By contributing to the planning phase the employee can offer valuable input in terms of what can and should be achieved and also is more likely to demonstrate ownership of and commitment to the performance management process.

Stage 2 – action

Once performance targets are agreed there will then follow a period in which the job is carried out. The degree to which the manager is involved in supporting and guiding performance during this period will depend on the individual and the circumstances of their job role. It is important that the manager is reasonably accessible and can provide ongoing coaching and feedback. There also may be others who have a role in supporting the individual in carrying out their role, such as other team members, and it is important that the manager facilitates such support.

Stage 3 – monitoring

As the individual carries out their job, their performance needs to be monitored to assess how they are performing against the performance targets. This is the period where data capture is very important. This is not just about identifying where there is a performance shortfall, but also about identifying strengths in performance. A holistic review of an individual's performance – one that captures information for accurate feedback and developmental purposes – is important here. Monitoring is also very important because the organization environment is not a static one – performance will be subject to new and changing demands, and objectives can lose relevance or feasibility. It is important to respond to these changes in a timely way.

Stage 4 – review

Reviews of performance should be ongoing, but there will also be more formal reviews of performance that may or may not be linked to pay decisions. Reviews enable the manager and employee to share information on progress towards performance targets. The aim of review is to support achievement of performance targets by identifying any action steps required as the job is carried out. To achieve this there needs to be a full and frank exchange of information. The manager needs to encourage upward feedback from individual employees on how they feel they are performing and also how well they feel the manager is supporting them in achieving their performance objectives.

The performance management cycle supports continuous improvement through an ongoing performance review, which captures data to use to drive improved performance moving forward. That may be from the situation of an employee underperforming who needs support to reach required standards, or it might be from the situation of a high-performing employee who needs fresh stretching targets and opportunities in order to grow and develop further. The performance management cycle therefore supports both the standards-orientated and excellence-orientated approaches to performance management.

A link can be made between the performance management cycle and Kolb's experiential model of learning (1985). A key element of Kolb's learning cycle is the opportunity to reflect on experiences. Monitoring and reviewing performance on an ongoing basis offers both the individual employee and the manager opportunities to reflect on performance. There should be opportunities to reflect on performance success, but also on those areas that are not meeting performance criteria. Dialogue on performance supports effective reflection and helps to create learning about how to improve performance moving forward.

Learning identified through monitoring and reviewing can then be applied back in the workplace with the aim of delivering improved performance moving forward. Given the time pressures in workplaces today, it is generally the ongoing monitoring and review that organizations struggle to deliver, as opposed to the initial objective setting or more formal performance review. It is important to keep driving home to line managers the importance of ongoing monitoring and review to provide timely feedback and to encourage the reflection and learning required to support continuous improvement.

The performance management cycle can also be found within the 'Investors in People Standard' framework. The standard aims to help participating organizations to transform business performance through people. It incorporates the key performance management stages of planning, taking action and evaluating and improving. Investors in People (IIP) provide many helpful case studies on their website (**www.investorsinpeople.com**) to demonstrate how committing to an investment in people that is aligned to your business goals can drive business performance. There is a clear recognition in the standard that, to be effective, performance management needs to be an ongoing cycle of activity not a once-a-year performance review.

The performance management cycle is not without its critics. It is argued by some that whilst the performance management cycle works well when it is operating within a fairly stable, established organization, it may not work so well in a rapidly changing environment, a small start-up organization or a company that has more of an emergent strategy than a classical strategy that is cascaded down from the top of the organization. I would argue that whilst the absence of an overarching holistic strategy might present issues in terms of aligning the planning process, the activities of ongoing monitoring and reviewing are hugely valuable activities when strategy is emerging in an iterative process.

Activity

- How well does your organization's practice fit the four stages of the performance management cycle identified above?

- Are there any stages of the cycle that work less well? Why do you think this is the case?

- What could be done to improve the effectiveness of each stage of the cycle?

- Is the performance management cycle an appropriate concept for your organization? If not, why not – and how might performance management be better structured?

Principles of good practice in performance management

As well as the basic principle of the ongoing, cyclical nature of performance management, the following are other principles that fairly consistently appear as factors linked to the success of an organization's performance management processes. This is intended as an overview, as some of these areas are explored in much greater depth in other areas of this book:

- *Clear purpose*

  Performance management should have clear aims and criteria on which the success of the process is judged. Performance management should contribute to the success of the organization and it is important that everyone understands what that contribution should be. Commitment to the process will be very difficult to achieve without stakeholders being able to identify a valuable output. Without a valuable output the question 'why bother?' is a reasonable one.

- *Visible commitment of senior managers*

  Effective performance management takes time and commitment from all stakeholders. Employees are unlikely to take the time or give the commitment to the performance management process if senior management in the organization are not role-modelling such commitment. When senior management are seen to be actively engaged with performance management, they are demonstrating that such activities are important and valued by the organization. In my experience it is very difficult to carry out performance management in such a way to add any value to an organization without authentic support and active engagement of the senior management team.

- *Line managers' ownership of the process*

  Performance management should not be owned by HR. Whilst they can provide expert advice and support, performance management needs to be owned and driven by the line managers who are responsible for managing individuals and teams. The implementation of performance management is explored in the next chapter, but it is worth highlighting here that early involvement by line managers in the design of the process, and support for them in terms of coaching or training so they have confidence in their ability to carry out the processes required, are vital elements in gaining that ownership.

- *Should apply to all staff*

  In the past some organizations chose to have performance management processes such as the performance review only for managerial staff and excluding manual workers. These practices are far less common today and there is a recognition that all employees should be part of an organization's performance management processes, including blue collar, secretarial and administrative staff. Even the CEO or MD of an organization can and should be included in performance management. I have been challenged on this, but whilst their performance aligns closely with the organization's results, it is also very particularly beneficial for them to receive peer and upward feedback as part of a performance review process.

- *Corporate goals translated into individual goals*

  Individuals should be working to goals that contribute to the success of the organization. It is important, therefore, that there is a clear connection between the goals set at an individual and team level and the wider goals of the organization. It is also important that the individual recognizes and understands how their role in the organization is contributing to its success.

- *Horizontal alignment*

  Performance management should not operate in a silo. To be effective it needs to be integrated with other areas of HRM to ensure a holistic approach to people management. This integrated approach has been explored in depth in the previous chapter.

- *Not command and control but consensus and empowerment*

  There should be partnership between employee and manager in the performance management process. There is little doubt that there is a role for direction and control within performance management to deliver alignment and the required standards of performance. However, the emphasis should be on achieving consensus and empowering the employee to deliver the required performance. It is important to achieve agreement between manager and employee in terms of what needs to be done and how it should be done. Employees who recognize the purpose and value in what they are doing, and feel they have the capability and support to deliver, are more likely to be motivated to meet the required performance. Employees who feel forced into performing in a certain way, who are unclear on the value or purpose of what they are doing, or feel they lack control over their own performance are much less likely to deliver the performance required and are unlikely to demonstrate any valuable discretionary behaviour. There may also be an impact on employee well-being, which may lead to performance problems such as absenteeism.

- *Supportive culture*

  The performance management process needs a supportive culture in order to be successful. In particular, a climate of trust and transparency is important to achieve the open dialogue that is so valuable in performance management (see Chapter 3 for a more in-depth exploration of culture).

- *Effectively resourced*

  Here the commitment of the organization and senior management to the process of performance management is key. Line managers need to be given the resources to ensure performance management can be carried out effectively. Those resources may include equipment or L&D interventions, but most importantly will include time – a commodity in high demand. There needs to be a recognition that performance management does and should take up the time of a line manager, and the line manager should feel that time given up to performance management is valued just as much by the organization as other responsibilities undertaken.

- *Forward-looking and developmental*

  Whilst the performance management process will need to review past performance, the main focus should be using that information to improve performance moving forward. It should provide a strong basis on which to develop performance, utilizing regular and frequent discussions between manager and employee.

- *Monitor and evaluation*

   Good practice in performance management requires the support of ongoing monitoring and evaluation of practices. To ensure it is delivering and will continue to deliver added value to the organization, it is vital that current practices are monitored and reviewed. Methods of carrying out this process are explored in greater detail in Chapter 8.

- *Continuous/evolutionary*

   Effective performance management is much more than an annual appraisal. To add true value it needs to be ongoing, and the review and feedback process should encourage learning that can be fed back into the process to encourage growth and improvement (the article below, by Clinton Wingrove, highlights the importance of the continuous nature of performance management).

Activity

Consider the principles of good practice in performance management (outlined above) in the context of your own organization. On a scale of 1–3, where 3 completely reflects good practice, 2 partly reflects best practice and 1 fails to reflect good practice, rate your organization against the principles identified. Once you have completed your review you may find it helpful to produce a SWOT (strengths, weaknesses, opportunities and threats) to reflect your organization's current standing in relation to best practice in performance management. From that SWOT, identify two or three areas you think your organization should focus on over the next 6 to 12 months to improve the way performance is managed. Provide a rationale for choices that you could present to a senior manager.

The following article brings to life some of the key themes in effective performance using the context of running a marathon.

'It's a marathon not a sprint'
By Clinton Wingrove

A week ago, London fell silent to pay tribute to those who lost their lives, and to those who were injured, in the Boston marathon bombing. Then, with enhanced vigour, some 36,000 athletes set off to meet their own personal challenges. There were no major international records broken but tens of thousands of individuals, most of whom will never even know each other, pulled together to make a collective statement and to achieve personal goals. Even those who did not finish are likely to have felt that they succeeded in some way.

But was it merely the goal of crossing the winning line or the reward of the medal at the finish line that made them run? No. The two most misunderstood concepts of traditional performance management are that (a) setting goals produces enhanced performance and (b) financial incentives maximize achievement of them.

There is no doubt that most top performers have clearly defined personal goals; the early finishers in London and Boston probably knew to the nearest 10 seconds the time they would take and were focusing on reducing that by mere seconds. But is that why they succeed? Probably not! Every single runner had a goal to finish as fast as they could – but many didn't or came in later than hoped.

We now know that it is not only the goal that matters – that merely provides the means of measurement. It is the belief in the value of the goal, the commitment to its achievement and the willingness to do what it takes to achieve it that are the key ingredients of success. And that is what we saw last week in the London Marathon: belief, commitment and a willingness to go the extra mile (sorry for the pun). But we also saw the results of many arduous months of unseen personally managed training, early morning runs, torn muscles, cramp, personal sacrifices and, for the many professional runners, minute attention to basic skill development supported by repetitive coaching; day after day after day.

Of course, the reward of the medal is immensely satisfying but does anyone believe that, when cramp strikes at the 20-mile marker, the medal is what makes people press on? Of course not! Even the professional runners, whose sponsorships can be impacted significantly, admit that it is their personal aspirations and reputation that drive them.

In business, we have to learn that effective leadership is needed to establish employee belief, commitment and willingness to apply discretionary effort. With that critical component, our staff will set and work to goals far higher than any we may dictate. During the year when they are working hard, struggling to go that extra mile or merely preparing for some later goal, we need to demonstrate that leadership and also provide effective management – enabling, guiding, encouraging and coaching them. Only then, will they put in and sustain the needed effort, practice their skills and believe that they can succeed – every single gruelling day.

To believe that annual goal setting, an infrequent performance appraisal and a few per cent annual pay increase will truly impact performance is as ridiculous as believing that I could win a marathon. Performance management simply isn't simple and needs to be done every single day.

SOURCE *People Management*, April 2013

The performance review

The performance review is a formal meeting to discuss an employee's performance. Many years ago a video was made by Video Arts company (now defunct) called *The Dreaded Appraisal*. It was an appropriate title, which seemed to encapsulate the way in which many managers and employees viewed the formal performance review meeting and review process. For many managers and employees the performance review is still seen, at best, as a necessary evil. Unfortunately, approached in this way the performance review is unlikely to deliver many – if any – positive outcomes for the employee, the manager or indeed the organization. The performance review process is more likely to be viewed positively when some clear valuable outcomes have been identified and when the review itself is conducted following good practice (as outlined below). It is also more likely to be successful when it is realistic in terms of what can be achieved.

The review is a general performance management tool and can be used for a variety of purposes such as increasing motivation or improving current performance. It works best when there are clear aims in place and the aims are realistic. If the review aims to achieve too much it is unlikely to succeed and may well cause confusion both for the employee and the manager.

Good practice in performance review

Planning

For a performance review to have any chance of valuable outcomes there needs to be adequate planning. Both the employee and the managers should be encouraged to capture key data relating to performance throughout the year, which can be discussed and explored during the formal review period. It is also important that both manager and employee are given enough time to prepare for the performance review meeting: how much time is enough time will depend on the organization and the role, but at least a week's notice should be given of an impending performance review meeting. During the period leading up to the meeting some key planning activities should take place:

- Sharing of last appraisal documentation and any objectives agreed at the last meeting (manager and employee to have a copy).

- An evaluation of performance against objectives agreed at last meeting (by both manager and employee) with data gathered to support evaluation.

- Sharing of the new blank appraisal form, so that the employee as well as the manager comes to the meeting with a draft evaluation of performance.

- Both parties should be encouraged to identify examples of good performance and also areas of performance where there might be developmental opportunities.

- Both parties should consider possible learning and development needs for the employee moving forward.

- The employee should be encouraged to identify helpful upward feedback for the manager.

These are fairly time-consuming activities, but when in place can help to ensure the performance review meeting is a two-way discussion, which can draw on strong evidence to support any performance evaluation and identify any action points moving forward. This is why a notification of a review a day in advance is clearly not sufficient.

Whilst issues relating to underperformance should be addressed in a timely basis – that is, not waiting for a formal performance review – it still may be the case that a manager needs to deliver some particularly difficult feedback or manage a difficult discussion with an employee. For example, in the situation where there is an employee who has been unwilling to accept previous feedback that has been given outside of the review relating to their underperformance, or an employee has struggled to address under-performance. In this situation, it can be very helpful for the manager to plan and rehearse how to deliver the feedback and/or manage the discussion. This is where HR can add value, providing coaching for the manager to help ensure that the feedback is delivered constructively and is more likely to lead to acceptance from the employee. It is much easier for HR to help a manager in advance than to become involved in a performance review meeting that has ended in argument and disagreement, and where the working relationship between manager and employee may have been damaged.

Time and location

Not only should enough time be set aside for planning a performance review, enough time should be set aside also for the meeting itself. Again, this isn't an exact science, but usually at least an hour is required for an effective performance review, particularly if it only happens once or twice a year. By allocating a reasonable amount of time to the meeting, the manager is communicating to the employee that they are valued and the process is considered to be important. For this reason it is also important not to move a performance review meeting unless it is absolutely unavoidable. If the meeting has to be moved it is important that the manager takes the time to explain personally to the employee the reasons for a reschedule. I know of one HR advisor who had his performance review meeting moved three times by his HR manager. This led to the HR advisor feeling very unappreciated and placed low in the manager's priorities. It put him in a very poor mindset for when the review meeting finally happened – and the review meeting was unsatisfactory for both parties as a result.

Usually an ideal location for a performance review is a meeting room. Not only will this help avoid any interruptions, but it also provides a neutral location, avoiding any status issues linked to using a manager's office. Meeting a manager sitting behind their own desk brings with it the danger of creating the teacher/pupil dynamic, which can have a very negative impact on the effectiveness of the performance review process. Open two-way communication is more likely to be achieved in a neutral, status-free zone. It is also the case that due to logistics relating to the geographical locations of appraiser and appraisee, reviews may not take place at the same location, but over the web. These reviews can work just as well as those taking place in the same room; however, checking the technology works beforehand and ensuring you are both in a confidential space are important considerations here.

Structure

The exact structure of the performance review meeting will depend on the context; however, there are some guiding principles here. First, it is a good idea to start by asking the employee to provide some self-assessment on his or her own performance. This can then provide a platform for the line manager to deliver their own evaluation of the employee's performance. Whilst the initial part of the review is an evaluation of past performance, it is important that the information generated by this discussion is used to move the review into a forward-looking position. The evaluation of past performance may include a review of performance against objectives set, a review of behavioural competencies and competencies developed.

The next stage of the review should look at how to develop the employee's performance moving forward. Part of this may involve areas of under-performance, or it might involve looking at how to create new stretching opportunities for an employee who is already performing to a high stand-ard. Again, this should be a two-way discussion and may involve problem solving, critical and creative thinking processes to generate ideas for grow-ing future performance.

Ideas generated at this point need to be translated into workable action points, or objectives should be agreed by the employee and line manager. In some situations it may be that the meeting needs an adjournment for both parties to review what has been discussed before a follow-up meeting is held to confirm agreed action points.

When an action plan is agreed, it is important that the plans are effectively resourced (time, money, equipment, learning and development interven-tions), to ensure that the individual has every opportunity to deliver against the performance required.

Some organizations will also incorporate a discussion on reward and/or career development with the performance review, but others will separate out such discussions into additional meetings. There is much debate regarding the pros and cons of integrating these areas, but it is certainly best not to try to achieve too much with a single meeting. One of the big criticisms of the performance review, in fact, is that in many cases it tries to achieve too much!

Documentation

It is very important that the manager brings relevant documentation to the meeting and ensures that the employee also has access to any relevant docu-mentation. This is where recording details of performance (good or poor) throughout the year is important in order to provide specific examples when discussing performance and providing feedback.

Closing the performance review

The manager must ensure that the employee is absolutely clear on what has been agreed and what the next steps and follow-up will be from the appraisal meeting. It is always best to end the review on a positive note, even where the employee may be underperforming or there may have been a degree of conflict or disagreement in the performance review meeting. The employee should leave the meeting feeling committed to the organization and with the belief that he or she is able to achieve the goals that have been set – and that he or she will be supported in doing so. Carried out well, a performance review should be a motivational tool.

Follow-up

It is important that the manager ensures there is a follow-up on the performance review. The timing of the follow-up will depend on the outcome of the performance review and the nature of the action points required. For example, if the outcome was the identification of an area of underperformance then it is very important that there is timely follow-up to ensure that resources to deal with the underperformance have been put in place and that performance is measured to assess any improvement. The employee will leave the performance review with a set of expectations. If these expectations are not met, there is very likely to be a negative impact on motivation and commitment of that employee. In my experience, the first four to six weeks after a performance review are critical in demonstrating to the employee that the performance review has been a useful process.

Follow-up is not just down to the line manager. The line manager needs the support of the organization and the HR department to ensure follow-through on action points. Line managers often become frustrated when they have made commitments to an employee in good faith and then the organization is slow to respond. This is where horizontal integration of people management activities is so important. A number of stakeholders may need involvement with the action points arising out of a performance review and it is vital that there are strong communications processes in place to ensure there is appropriate follow-up.

Interpersonal skills required for carrying out the performance review

As with all areas of line management, to conduct an effective performance review meeting the manager is required to demonstrate a strong set of interpersonal skills. The manager needs to demonstrate clarity and objectivity in all forms of communication during the appraisal interview. As a general rule, particularly when delivering constructive criticism, it is much better to get straight to the point and be direct rather than to cushion comments in language that may confuse the employee. There are some particular areas where a robust skill set will help ensure an effective performance review:

- *Effective questioning*

  As with selection interviewing, principles of good practice in questioning are important for the appraisal interview. In some cases the appraiser will need to use closed questions requiring a straight yes or no response, for example, when requiring clarification or control such as bringing a line of questioning to a close. However, to achieve a good two-way dialogue it is important that a range of open questions are asked. For example, 'What factors do you believe contributed to that customer complaint?' Probing questions enable the appraiser to explore initial responses in more depth. Such questions often use a behavioural style, for example, 'Tell me more about that customer complaint, what did you say in response?' Often a funnelling approach to questioning works well, starting with an open question, probing further and then ending with a closed question, for example, 'So overall you would say you were happy with the way you handled that customer complaint?'

  There are certain styles of questioning that should be avoided in the performance review. For example, leading questions that direct the appraisee towards giving you the response you are looking for rather than giving an honest response from their own perspective. Also multiple questions, as asking more than one question at a time can cause confusion and not elicit clear responses.

- *Effective listening and observation skills*

  It is important that the manager has a clear understanding of what the appraisee is saying during the performance review and also what they are not saying! I have witnessed performance reviews where both parties have left the meeting with very different views of the discussion and this is then highlighted when the review is written up for agreement. It is important that during the performance review the manager reflects back to the employee his or her understanding of what the employee is saying and gives the employee the opportunity to confirm or offer more clarification where needed. Using wording such as, 'So what you are telling me is that...' or, 'So to summarize, we have agreed that...' will help ensure that effective listening has taken place and that there is a shared understanding of what has been agreed.

Observation skills are also very important. People can show by their facial expressions and body language things that they may not be vocalizing. For example, it is important to look for signs that an employee is unhappy, withholding information or feeling defensive. Avoiding eye contact is a typical sign of withholding information and lack of transparency; however, cultural differences should be taken into consideration here. Crossed arms are a typical sign of defensiveness and may indicate that the employee is unhappy or insecure with the direction that the performance review is taking.

Another factor to consider is that silence does not signpost agreement. There is a temptation when faced with silence to move on to another discussion point, or to dive in to fill the silence without giving the employee time to respond. What managers need to do is to persist in encouraging the silent employee to offer a response. This may well lead to an uncomfortable period of silence; sometimes an employee needs the space and time to gather their thoughts before responding to a question.

- *Effective feedback skills*

  Feedback is explored in much greater depth in Chapter 6, but it is important to state here that it forms a crucial part of an effective performance review. Constructive feedback based on objective evidence is what is required; the feedback should be given against a backdrop of ongoing feedback so that there shouldn't be any big surprises in the feedback given. The feedback should also be two-way, with the employee being encouraged to provide upward feedback to the line manager during the review.

- *Conflict resolution*

  Disagreement may well occur during the performance review process, and indeed a certain amount of conflict or disagreement may actually benefit the review by ensuring a full and open discussion of issues of relevance. It is important that any conflict is managed constructively and not allowed to damage the employment relationship moving forward. There are various approaches to managing conflict. One often-referenced classical approach to conflict management is that of Ruble and Thomas (1976), which outlines five strategies to handle conflict:

  - Competition: here the manager would take a very assertive, telling approach in which they would win and the employee would lose any point of disagreement. This strategy would need to be considered carefully as the exercise of power in a win/lose approach carries the danger of damaging the employment relationship moving forward. However, there may be a time when such an approach is appropriate. For example, perhaps an employee has been refusing to regularly wear a piece of safety equipment and still, in the performance review, refuses to accept it as a requirement of carrying out their job. In this situation it is likely to be appropriate for the manager to insist that this needs to happen moving forward.

– Avoidance: this is where the manager would choose to move on from the conflict without any resolution taking place. It may be that the conflict is taking up too much time in the review, or that further information is needed, or that emotions are becoming heightened. In any of these cases, it might be appropriate to take the area of conflict out of the performance review discussion to be addressed at another time.

– Accommodation: here the manager is unassertive in their view or aims and the employee achieves what they want from the area where there is some conflict. This might be appropriate when the issue of conflict is of far greater importance to the employee than the manager – and the manager recognizes that for the sake of an ongoing positive relationship it might be reasonable to give way on this particular point.

– Compromise: here the manager and the employee find a middle ground between their two points of view that enables a way forward. This may be a good solution, but this is not always the case. Sometimes a compromise results in a poor decision being made and leaves both parties feeling dissatisfied with the final outcome.

– Collaboration: is seen to be one of the most effective ways of approaching the management of conflict. Here the manager and the employee work together through the areas of disagreement. Problem solving, creative thinking and sharing of information are all activities that may be appropriate in this approach. This strategy for dealing with conflict is more likely to achieve long-term positive outcomes – a win/win.

- *Emotional intelligence*

As a concept emotional intelligence was brought to prominence by Daniel Goleman (1998), who felt that the classical viewpoint of intelligence was too narrow and that the emotional qualities of individuals were an important factor in performance at work, particularly the performance of leaders in the workplace. The concept of emotional intelligence is generally broken down into four areas:

- Self-awareness: having a good sense of self, strengths and weakness.
- Self-management: understanding what we are feeling and why and managing those feelings effectively.
- Social-awareness: having empathy for others, being able to read how others are feeling and respond appropriately.
- Relationship management: effective influencing, leadership, conflict management and ability to build teamwork and collaborative working.

Emotional intelligence has an important role to play in the effective performance review, enabling the fostering of a positive manager/employee relationship and encouraging employee engagement with the process. Careful consideration of how the employee might be feeling about his or her performance and the performance review – the ability to empathize, will help the manager prepare effectively for the performance review and carry it out in such a way that both parties leave feeling positive.

CASE STUDY

A charity based in the East End of London had introduced a formal performance review process about 12 months previously. The organization had been growing quite rapidly and it had become clear that a structured process needed to be put into place. Beyond objective setting and feedback, the HR director also hoped that the performance review process would ensure that underperformance was more effectively addressed by line managers. A year into implementation, the HR director was concerned that, despite having a formal process in place, underperformance was still not being addressed. Typical performance review forms came back with managers having given satisfactory or above ratings for performance, when often the employee was not fully meeting his or her objectives or the overall performance requirements of the role. The HR director decided to conduct some structured interviews with a selection of her line managers in order to explore what the issues might be.

Early on in the interviewing process a clear pattern of feedback was emerging. The line managers demonstrated a strong desire to avoid conflict and maintain harmony within their teams. They felt very uncomfortable taking any action that might lead to conflict, or that might distress a member of their team. They also appeared to lack confidence in some of the interpersonal skills required to address underperformance.

The managing director of the organization had a highly paternalistic management style and had created a culture that made all employees feel they were part of a family at work. There were strong benefits to this sense of family, such as a high degree of support and positive feedback provided to fellow employees, and very cohesive teams. However, the culture was also causing problems, creating an environment where consensus was becoming an overriding goal and conflict was avoided at the expense of a healthy airing of views. Reviewing in depth how the performance reviews were conducted, it became clear to the HR director that many reviews focused purely on areas of success, while more problematic areas were not discussed at all.

For the organization to achieve its performance objectives moving forward, it was clear to the HR director that it wasn't only the line managers' conduct of performance reviews that needed to change, but there needed to be a degree of cultural and behavioural change as well. The HR director and the senior management team decided to focus initially on identifying and then developing some core behaviours both for themselves and for the other line managers in the organization that would drive change. These behaviours included: individuals having the courage to challenge others, actively encouraging others to challenge them, and regularly providing constructive criticism when needed. Behavioural and cultural change takes time, but the need for change was explained to all in the organization, and support and development were provided as the organization gradually adapted.

With regard to the performance review process, managers were encouraged to address underperformance throughout the year and not leave any discussion to the formal performance review. In a climate where there was a greater acceptance of the need to challenge and to provide timely, constructive feedback to address problem areas, the managers felt more comfortable addressing performance areas where there was the potential of a degree of conflict with those they managed.

In addition, managers were given training in the areas of conflict management and giving feedback. As well as the desire to maintain harmony, managers had also been avoiding discussions relating to underperformance because they felt ill-equipped to deliver the feedback required and unsure about how to manage any potential conflict that might ensue.

It was a gradual process, but the HR director reported one year down the line that the performance review forms now mostly provided a more honest, holistic reflection of the performance of the employee.

The future of the annual performance review and rethinking performance management

When writing the first edition of this book several years ago, I referenced the growing debate regarding the value of the annual performance review or appraisal. This debate has really grown in more recent years with several high-profile organizations axing annual performance reviews (for example, Adobe and Accenture) and related ranking systems. Organizations such as Microsoft and Deloitte have shifted their approach to performance management to focus on more regular performance discussions. A brief search on the internet will produce a range of examples of articles claiming the death of the annual appraisal, or challenging organizations to axe the 'dreaded' annual appraisal. Many organizations are now rethinking their approach to performance management.

However, a recent CIPD Research Report (2016a) explores whether there really has been a 'Performance Management Revolution' and suggests that:

> Despite the strong rhetoric, it quickly becomes apparent that – perhaps no surprise – the headlines are often overstatements and the suggested revolution is nothing like as great in reality.

The implication here is that for many organizations there is an evolution in performance management rather than a seismic shift.

Before making the decision to move away from a focus on the annual performance review, you should consider the case for change and some of the challenges involved as outlined below. At the end of this section there is an activity which outlines some areas for consideration when exploring changing your approach to performance management.

The case for change

As previously discussed, the pace of change in the world of work and wider society appears greater than ever before. A reliance on an annual appraisal means that objectives may lose currency quickly, may no longer be relevant or may be met well in far shorter time frames than 12 months. You are likely to have heard employees and managers alike who have talked about forgotten objectives lying in a virtual file, pulled out once a year and rarely, if at all, reviewed in between. This will do little to support organizations seeking performance aligned to organization goals, agility and innovation.

Less able managers may leave giving feedback (positive or negative) to that annual discussion as they know this is the only time it will be tracked or formally required for reporting purposes. Meanwhile, there is a growing hunger and expectation in the workplace for timely feedback and support, such as through a variety of learning and development interventions. This is a trend that has been identified particularly amongst younger employees entering the workplace who are used to having access to real-time information and response. Those organizations with a reliance mainly on the annual appraisal may well struggle in meeting this need.

Also, for many organizations the annual appraisal has become weighed down in a sea of bureaucratic 'paperwork', which managers and employees alike have found time-consuming, unnecessarily complex and perhaps most damning of all – lacking in any clear positive output. For some organizations there has been so much focus on the task of ensuring x per cent of annual appraisals were completed on time, that the key stakeholders lost sight of why they were being done in the first place.

It is therefore perhaps no surprise that some organizations have started to question the value of the annual performance review.

The challenges

Removal of the annual performance review – or shifting away from such a heavy reliance on this tool – is not without its challenges. Organizations have shown they are not insurmountable, but they need to be considered when reviewing your approach. Firstly, there is the challenge of time. Managers already argue that they don't have the time to do annual appraisals. Arguably, regular check-ins can require even more time, so organizations need to be prepared to give managers the time and resources to deliver. Linked to this is line manager capability. Managers need to be equipped with the skills to manage performance on an ongoing basis without the more formal structure provided by the annual appraisal. Removing the annual review can place even more responsibility on the employee to take ownership of their own performance. This isn't necessarily a bad thing, but it does mean that an employee needs the capability and related confidence to do this. A shift away from the annual appraisal therefore needs careful consideration of resourcing issues.

Shifting away from the formal setting of the annual performance review may also create challenges in tracking performance, particularly underperformance. Again, this isn't insurmountable, but you need to consider what data you do need to be capturing on performance and how you will do this moving forward. This is particularly important when justifying decisions relating to reward. Many annual appraisal schemes have led to the output of a rating linked to a reward outcome. We explore ratings in more depth later in this book but whatever the decision on the link between performance and reward, outcomes must be based on fair, objective criteria.

The value moving forward

My personal conclusion is that the annual performance review or appraisal isn't dead yet and in fact doesn't necessarily need to die, but performance management shouldn't rely on this once-a-year focus on performance. The annual review should always be seen as just one element of the wider performance management process and should always be placed in the context of ongoing review and feedback (CIPD, 2017b). When done well, as outlined earlier in this chapter, it can offer real benefit to employee, manager and the organization. I think an opportunity to stop and reflect on performance over the longer term can offer an objective, holistic view on performance, which can then build into planning performance and personal development over the medium term. It avoids the danger of just relying purely on 'a snapshot in time', which may not be truly reflective of how an employee is generally performing. It should be an opportunity to capture and celebrate the achievements of the employee and motivate the employee moving forward. An annual review supported with regular check-ins to review objectives, provide timely feedback and revise plans as required can support effective performance in organizations.

However, as ever, I would recommend that the actual approach you take should reflect the particular needs and nature of your organization. There are good practices to adopt, both keeping or discarding the annual performance review and as with the wider performance management process, I recommend you aim to bring insight in and then shape the right solution for your organization. A sound knowledge of your organization and the external environment it operates in will be key factors in enabling you to do that.

CASE STUDY Interview with Anila DeHart, Deloitte

Anila DeHart is a Priority Leader in Global Talent focusing on the Deloitte Global Performance Experience, Cognitive Insights and Knowledge Curation. Deloitte have been leading the way in rethinking performance management and have rolled out a transformational approach to more than 200,000 practitioners worldwide. In March 2018, I interviewed Anila to learn more about the journey travelled so far.

What were the key drivers that led to a shift in the approach to managing performance at Deloitte?

There's never been a better time to rethink talent processes than now. A number of external and internal drivers and research helped build the case for change and inform the new approach. A couple of areas to highlight:

Talent trends and research

The expectations of talent have changed dramatically. Today's and future talent expect more frequent honest feedback, opportunities to leverage strengths, greater clarity in how to meet professional and personal goals, and more opportunities to learn and grow.

However, the traditional end-of-year appraisal, designed in the 1970s, is not designed to meet these expectations and clearly isn't effective anymore. In 2015, the Deloitte Global Human Capital Trends research showed that 82 per cent of companies reported that performance evaluations 'were not worth the time' (Deloitte, 2015). In addition, long-term research by Gallup studied 1.4 million individuals in high-performing teams across 192 organizations and highlighted the importance of a strengths-based performance and a development approach to increase engagement and performance (Buckingham and Coffman, 1999).

Internal factors

Within our organization, employee, business leader and talent feedback evidenced that the old process, including ratings, were demotivating our talent and didn't drive improvement in performance. Further evidence of the need for change came from a study with more than 60 high-performing Deloitte teams, comparing them to a baseline that included approximately 2,000 employees, which highlighted that key enablers of high-performing teams were: strengths-based development, frequent feedback and clarity about expectations.

What have been the key changes made?

We responded by fundamentally rethinking how we do performance. This started with broadening the objectives of the performance approach. We expanded the goal from 'recognize' performance (annual activities that allow intelligent compensation, promotion and low-performer management decisions) to also include 'seeing' and 'fuelling' performance.

Through focus on 'seeing' performance, we aim to generate rich and ongoing data that gives the business leaders a more complete view into the performance of their teams to inform performance improvement, redeployment and upskilling decisions. On the other hand, 'fuelling' performance drives a shift from activities targeted to performance management and process to activities that focus on ongoing and balanced feedback.

We enabled these objectives through an agile and user-friendly design, which includes a number of complimentary components. Two key components of the new design are:

- *Check-ins*: We introduced frequent, future-focused conversations about the work. Here, team members and team leaders meet one to one to explore real-time feedback and expectations for the near-term work. It's how they align on priorities for what's coming next, and they do that with a strengths lens. They discuss how the individual will deliver on these priorities given their unique skills and strengths, and how the team leader will create opportunities for them to do that. We called them frequent, but we didn't mandate a frequency. We left this up to business leaders to communicate as they saw fit. Today, the majority of our people are doing them either weekly or biweekly. We also didn't require anyone to document anything going into or coming out of a check-in. *We didn't want anything to stand in the way of the conversation.* We stressed that the logistics of check-ins are not as important as making them a habit. The tone, nature and content of a check-in should evolve over time and reflect the needs of each individual, project and project phase. Our people who were used to heavy documentations once or twice per year were now expected to shift that time to where the work—the performance—was happening in real time. Check-ins are now part of how our people get their work done.

- *Performance snapshots*: Moving away from ratings didn't mean we'd stop capturing performance data. Performance snapshots are one of several ways we now capture data and are a vehicle for the team leader to capture his or her assessment about each team member's performance, at a moment in time. Snapshots are timely, completed at the end of a project, phase or at least quarterly, allowing team leaders to capture their judgement of performance as close as possible to when it occurs. By the end of the year, there are numerous snapshots completed for each person, and coupled with other data such as metrics, training received, etc, they provide a rounded view of our people's performance.

  Snapshots are research-based. Rather than ask leaders to rate the skills of others, we've crafted questions that ask them to rate their own intended future actions. This approach counteracts the idiosyncratic rater effect, which research has shown distorts ratings because the main variable is the evaluator. Leaders in the new system make decisions based on what they know about a team member's performance instead of what they think of the person.

Snapshots are easy. Our performance snapshots use four questions, answered on a Likert-type scale, so no more paragraphs to write! The snapshots can even be completed on smartphones to make these as simple as possible for our on-the-go workforce, to enable an ongoing flow of data throughout the year.

I've only covered two features here, but our approach also includes:

- *Scatterplots*, which represent an aggregate view of performance snapshot data and other metrics and are made available to team members on a regular basis to enable transparency and prompt more focused feedback discussions.
- *Team pulse surveys*, which provide team leaders with insights about the engagement of their teams to drive team conversations around how to increase it.
- *Career coach* who helps employees discover their strengths, find more ways to leverage them, explore performance trends and develop their careers.
- *Talent reviews* in which leaders discuss development needs of select talent segments.
- *Quarterly business reviews*, which are analytics-driven leader reviews of the 'health' of their teams to inform talent actions and decisions.

What have been the challenges involved with this shift in approach?

- Embedding the new behaviours requires change management and doesn't happen overnight. Behaviours (such as shying away from honest feedback and hiding behind documentation and ratings) take time to change and we needed to ensure the change continues to be a priority even after deployment.
- While reward and promotion remain local processes, the talent teams in each of the countries needed to ensure a seamless link of the performance outputs with the local year-end processes. This required additional local HR resource capacity to design, socialize and communicate the link.

- Developing and deploying globally a home-grown tool and analytics solution required significant investment and governance – we would have preferred to leverage an 'off the shelf' solution, but the available tools didn't meet the requirements of our new approach at the time of deployment.

What have been the key learnings so far?

- An iterative approach helps with adoption and enhancements – we've pursued a measured testing and implementation approach, rather than a big bang.
- Benefits increase with more time on the experience; we learn and adapt the more we embed these changes. It is therefore really important to track progress and also communicate the benefits and success stories to increase confidence in and support for the changes made.

So what's next?

Our approach has evolved over the initial pilots and also during the last two years of deploying the approach to 80 per cent of our global population, and it will likely continue to evolve as we expand and learn.

Next up, we will dial up our focus on optimization and embedding the change. This phase puts a focus on creating stronger behaviours and a strengths mindset and continuing to develop the team leader and coach skills and insights to fuel performance and engagement.

This next phase also includes continued innovation to the experience and enabling tools, particularly around leveraging analytics and cognitive insights to drive the right behaviours.

Any final words of advice for organizations shifting their focus away from the annual appraisal?

Because the old approach is likely to be so rooted in processes and entrenched behaviours, expect resistance at the start of the journey. Prepare for this and consider strategies to gain acceptance and support. To have any real chance of success, the change needs to be strongly sponsored by your business leaders and linked to the overall culture change.

Activity

If you are considering moving away from a focus on an annual performance review in your organization, here are some initial considerations:

- How well is your current approach working? Seek feedback from key stakeholders here to analyse strengths and weaknesses. If your approach is working well don't feel you have to change just because others have.

- Conduct some external research. Explore what other organizations have done and seek out evidence of successful impact and difficulties encountered. Would these approaches suit your organization, its culture, size, structure for example?

- What resourcing requirements are needed and can they be met by your organization? For example, time requirements and capability of managers and employees. Is the time right for change or do you need to build underpinning resources first?

- What data do you need to capture, track and report on for performance management? How will you do this if you change the current approach?

- What is your current reward strategy and how will changing your approach to the performance review and associated ratings impact on that?

In this chapter we explored principles of best practice in performance management. We looked in depth at the performance review as a subset of the performance management process. We identified activities and behaviours, including the interpersonal skills of the manager, which contribute to an effective performance review that leads to positive outcomes for the employee, the manager and the organization.

In the next chapter we look more closely at how to implement performance management in an organization, considering some of the practical action steps that need to be taken and identifying potential barriers that may need to be overcome.

DIAGNOSTIC QUESTIONNAIRE

Using a sample of employees from your organization, evaluate their experiences of the performance review process (see Table 4.1). The larger the sample you can achieve, the clearer picture you will have of the typical employee experience of the process. You may discover patterns relating to seniority of employees, or variations between functional areas of the organization – and these may warrant further investigation. You also may find it helpful to adapt the questions and use them with a sample of managers to see if the feedback is similar (in my experience, managers often leave the performance review meeting with a much more positive impression of how the review process went than that of the employee!). For example, question one could be, 'Do I give those I manage sufficient time to prepare effectively for performance review meetings?'.

TABLE 4.1 Evaluating the performance review in your organization

On a scale of 1–5 where 1 is 'strongly disagree' and 5 is 'strongly agree', rate your experience of your performance review.
1   I was given enough notice to prepare for the performance review. 1   2   3   4   5
2   I was given a copy of my previous objectives and the last review to enable me to prepare effectively for the review. 1   2   3   4   5

(continued)

TABLE 4.1 (*Continued*)

3 My manager had supporting evidence/data to support feedback regarding my performance. 1 2 3 4 5
4 The discussion was two-way and I was able to provide a self-assessment of my performance. 1 2 3 4 5
5 I was able to give my managers feedback on how well I feel they have supported me in achieving my performance targets. 1 2 3 4 5
6 My learning and development needs were discussed during the performance review. 1 2 3 4 5
7 A learning and development plan has been identified to meet my learning and development needs. 1 2 3 4 5
8 I feel my manager allocated sufficient time for the performance review. 1 2 3 4 5
9 I am happy with the outcomes of the performance review. 1 2 3 4 5
10 How could your experience of the performance review be improved moving forward?

How do you do it?

05

This chapter explores the activities and challenges involved in implementing a performance management process in an organization. The theories relating to good practice explored in the previous chapter are valuable in terms of guiding us as to 'how' performance management should be carried out – this chapter focuses on the practicalities of developing, designing and implementing a performance management process. This can be costly in terms of time and money, so it is very important that it is carried out efficiently and effectively.

Whilst every organization situation will present different issues and challenges for those charged with developing and implementing a performance management process, there are some key stages and activities that are likely to have relevance and value to many organizational situations. It is helpful to break down development and implementation into three stages: first, the planning and analysis stage, the large part of which is information gathering and then analysis of that data to identify an appropriate and practical way forward. Second, the design stage when more detail with regards to the content and processes involved in performance management are agreed. Third, the implementation stage, the rolling out of performance management; effective project management skills are of great importance here. However, the starting point is ensuring that there is effective leadership of the process, providing both direction and control, but most importantly involving and gaining the commitment of the stakeholders in the performance management process. Who should lead the process of delivering a new or changed performance management process into an organization and what is required of that leadership?

Leading the process

Who should lead the process?

As with any process of development and implementation it is very important that it is led effectively. In terms of who is charged with leading the process of developing and implementing a performance management process this can vary between organizations. Where there is a significant HR presence in an organization then often the head of HR or the HR director will lead the process, usually working closely with one or more members of the senior management team. However, in other organizations it may be that a senior line manager with significant people management responsibilities may lead the project, working with HR, or in other cases an external consultant may be used working with a member of senior management.

Where the process is led by HR, it is very important that the process of performance management is not seen as an HR initiative but a business initiative, a process embedded in the wider organization to drive business performance. This is easier against a backdrop where HR is already seen as business-focused and where there is HR representation at a senior level within the organization. Where HR has a less strategic role in the organization, there may be challenges in influencing senior management to gain their commitment to the process. Leadership from HR should ensure that the process utilizes knowledge of good practice in performance management in order to maximize the impact on, and added value to, the organization.

Where the process is led by a senior line manager, it is important that they are fully aware of good practice in performance management. Where they are not, it may be appropriate to use the expertise of an HR manager (or similar) within the organization, who may not have the seniority to lead the project but who can operate as an advisor to the senior manager, bringing specific HR knowledge and skill to the process. Here, HR is operating as an HR advisor rather than as a change agent to the process (Storey, 1992).

Where an external consultant is used it is very important that the understanding of context (as discussed below) is achieved. Consultants can bring significant expertise, experience and objectivity not available in-house, but there is the danger of a generic solution being identified that is not supported by the realities of the organizational context. Good consultants come with strong references, and a willingness to listen to what the client has to say. However, organizations need to remember that working with consultants is a two-way process. To be able to provide effective solutions, consultants need to have appropriate access to information in order to provide tailored approaches to organization needs. If they are not given access to the information they need then they are unlikely to deliver effectively against any client brief. Ideally the relationship between the organization and the consultant should be one based on collaboration and such collaboration requires high levels of mutual trust and open communication from both parties in order to operate most effectively.

What should the leader of the process provide?

Much of the process of developing and implementing a performance management process is about taking the organization through change. So many of the leadership qualities required for effective change management have relevance here:

- identifying and communicating a clear vision;
- providing a rationale for change;
- exploring barriers to change and strategies to overcome those barriers;
- gaining commitment behind the change and identifying change agents to support change;
- transparent, regular communication during change;
- demonstrating a willingness to take feedback on board.

What style of leadership is likely to be most effective?

In terms of the most appropriate leadership style, in many cases a transformational and participative leadership style is likely to be most effective and lead to positive outcomes. Transformation leaders provide a vision and work with others collaboratively to gain the involvement and commitment required to achieve the vision. Participative leadership, involving stakeholders in the process of developing and designing a process, has been shown to be more successful in achieving the commitment and support of those stakeholders at the point of implementation and on an ongoing basis. However, as Goleman (2000) has argued, it may be that at different times during the project life cycle different styles of leadership are required, and also recognizing that there may be a wide range of stakeholders; it may be necessary for the leaders to 'flex' their style to the particular context. Goleman (2000) identifies six leadership styles and argues that leaders with the best results do not rely on just one leadership style, but can comfortably use four more of the styles in order to respond appropriately to the needs of a particular situation. The six styles Goleman adopts are as follows:

- coercive style – leader demands complete compliance;
- authoritative style – leader mobilizes people towards a vision;
- affiliative style – leader creates emotional bonds and harmony;
- democratic style – leader uses participation to build consensus;

- pacesetting style – leader expects excellence and self-direction from followers;
- coaching style – leader develops people for the future.

Activity

- Consider some of the key stages of a project and the activities that a project leader might be involved with. The project might be implementing a performance management process, but you may find it helpful to use an example of another project you have recently been involved with at work.

- Now think about the range of stakeholders (their seniority, skill and knowledge set, personalities, interest in the project) that might be involved with a project.

- Review Goleman's six leadership styles and think of one or two examples of situations where it might be appropriate for that particular leadership style to be adopted.

- Why do you think that that leadership style is more likely to lead to positive outcomes in that situation?

- Why might another style used in that situation be problematic?

There would appear to be a clear role for the authoritative, affiliative and democratic styles of leadership in developing and implementing a performance management process. Providing a clear vision, creating positive teamworking and involving stakeholders are each important in this situation. A coaching style may also be required; for example, in supporting stakeholders to be effective participants in the performance management process. When dealing with a confident and able team it may be that a pace-setting style is appropriate, but used in the wrong circumstances it can overwhelm employees. A demand for excellence at a time when employees are struggling to achieve good practice can cause stress and impact on motivation. At face value, a coercive style may seem inappropriate for most circumstances, but there may be times when discussion or argument needs to end, and a decision needs to be made. Indeed stakeholders may look to the project leaders for a decision when an impasse has been reached, even though that decision may be unpopular with some. A coercive style used on an ongoing basis is unlikely to lead to positive outcomes. It is likely to lead to a lack of true engagement with the project and has the potential to damage ongoing relationships.

There is much debate regarding the degree to which a leader can 'flex' their style of leadership. Certainly at a basic level, the ability to respond appropriately to the needs of a situation, the task at hand and those employees being led, is likely to be valuable to a leader taking an organization through the implementation of a new or adapted process. It may also be that different members of the project team may step up into a leadership role when their particular style of leading can really add some value.

Identifying change agents

Early on in the process it is useful to identify key 'influencers' in the organization who can help drive through implementation and support the change process. The actual position of these employees in the organization (in terms of seniority) is irrelevant. It could be that in the organization's formal hierarchy they are actually quite junior. These 'influencers' are people who shape opinion in the organization, they are people who employees listen to; they have their views respected and yield considerable personal power in the organization as a result. These may be the very individuals who are most resistant to any new or changed performance management system, but being aware of who they are and working hard from an early stage to gain their involvement in and commitment to the process is very valuable. Once on board with the process they can offer considerable support to those leading the project in terms of gaining commitment across the wider organization.

Development: planning and analysis

Context

The development and implementation of a performance management process typically starts with an exploration of context. Chapter 3 considers in depth how performance management should 'fit' with the organizational context and it is worth revisiting some of the themes identified, as they are of particular importance when developing a performance management process.

Organization culture

A performance management process is more likely to stand a chance of delivering valuable outcomes when it fits with the culture and the core values of the organization. Encouraging behaviours within the performance management process that do not reflect the values of the organization is likely to lead to frustration and conflict. For example, if part of the new process is designed to encourage innovation, yet the culture of the organization is one of caution and risk-averse, the performance management process is highly unlikely to be successful. I would caveat that by highlighting that the performance management system may well be a key element in driving cultural change in the organization. As long as there is strong senior leadership commitment to the overall goals and an appreciation that things may be 'a little bumpy' during the transition, a mismatch with current culture may not be a problem in the short term. It is important, therefore, to have a strong sense of the culture and values of an organization when shaping the performance management process. It may be that the culture of the organization is fairly obvious, but in some cases a more structured approach of observation, interviews and focus groups may be required to gain a true sense of culture and the typical behaviours evident in the organization.

Management style

Closely linked to the culture of the organization is the prevailing management style. A performance management process that encourages two-way communication, aims to deliver consensus and empower employees will struggle against a backdrop where authoritarianism is the prevailing management style. If there is a recognition that cultural change and a change in management style is required by the organization, it makes sense for some progress to be made on that before attempting a performance management process based on consensus and empowering employees. As with culture, the prevailing management style may be fairly evident, but structured observation and interviewing/focus groups may help in gaining a true picture.

Organization type and structure

The nature of the organization, the structure and the work processes will all influence both what is achievable and what is likely to add value in performance management terms. Armstrong (2009: 260) writes: 'Structural considerations will also affect the way in which performance management is introduced. In a highly decentralized organization, or one in which authority is devolved to some functions or divisions, it may be appropriate to encourage or permit each unit or function to develop its own approach to performance management as long as it conforms to central guidelines or basic principles.'

There are particular challenges in introducing a standardized performance management process in an organization that operates in many different countries. The need for consistency and standardization must be balanced against the unique circumstances of each country and be particularly sensitive to the cultural differences.

Complex matrix structures, very hierarchical structures, or organizations with a wide 'span of control' (the number of subordinates reporting directly to a manager) all present particular considerations for the design and implementation of performance management. For example, where managers have a very wide span of control it may be necessary to consider carefully what is realistic for them to achieve in terms of performance managing their direct reports. Any process must be realistic in terms of the time required of any individual manager – and managers are more likely to fully engage with the process when they believe that the time they need to devote to the process is recognized and valued by the organization.

Historical backdrop

Understanding the historical backdrop to performance management within the organization is of value here. In some situations there may have been no performance management process before, but in other situations many performance management processes may have been tried in the past with varying degrees of success. Previous experiences of performance management processes will have shaped employee opinion towards it and will influence how they view any new initiative. Negative experiences may have left considerable cynicism and some work may be required to achieve attitudinal change. Consider the following scenario.

Scenario

George has worked for ABC Engineering for nearly 20 years. For the last 10 years he has worked in management and is currently a section head in charge of a department of 30 employees. Since George has been with ABC Engineering there have been six different performance management processes introduced, starting with a very basic process when he first joined, to the latest version that includes a competency framework and 360-degree feedback. The personnel director has called together the 10 section heads in the organization to explain the latest process and deal with any questions they have; his aim is to gain their full commitment. The personnel director finishes his presentation and asks for comments/questions and George puts his hand up:

This is the sixth performance management process I have seen introduced into ABC. In my experience there is a lot of fuss, time and energy spent on these launches. We get briefings and then get sent off on a one-day training course and then we are just left to get on with it. Everyone is enthusiastic initially, but it always ends up the same way. No real value comes out of the process, particularly the performance review, which we complete and it then sits in an electronic file in the personnel system with nothing happening. I have put loads of requests in for training for my team as a result of performance reviews and absolutely nothing happens. Gradually, me and my team and everyone else involved in the process loses interest and we go back to giving daily directions and informal feedback, until of course you guys come up with yet another version for us all to try. It takes up a huge amount of my time and, to be honest, I think that time will be better used elsewhere on activities that actually contribute to my section targets where there is a clear valuable outcome!

Multiply that scenario by a few section heads and suddenly you sense the real challenge that this personnel director faces in order to win the hearts and minds of the section heads to support the new process. This scenario and the line manager's mindset are not that unusual. Ideally the personnel director would have involved the section heads earlier on in the process rather than presenting a fait accompli, but beyond that, this scenario highlights the importance of understanding the historical backdrop. Understanding what has happened before in terms of performance management and recognizing how that may have shaped opinions. Understanding how people in the organization are likely to respond to the launch of a performance management process will help those leading the initiative to prepare for the likely responses and have strategies and arguments to lead and manage the required change effectively.

Activity

Put yourself in the position of the personnel director at ABC Engineering and consider the following questions:

- How might you respond to George's viewpoint?

- What might you do to influence George to change his attitude towards the new process?

- What could you have done before the meeting to reduce the likelihood of responses such as George's being presented?

Whatever the historical backdrop to performance management in the organization, it is important that a strong understanding of context is achieved as a backdrop to any decisions that are made regarding the way forward and that stakeholder support is achieved early on in the process.

External research

When deciding on your organization's approach to performance management it is important to do your research beyond the organization as well as within. That doesn't mean finding out what your more successful competitor does and adopting that, as what works for them may be completely wrong for your organization. What it does mean is ensuring that you explore what options are available and seek out a range of relevant case study organizations that have success stories to share. This is where networks are invaluable, not just for performance management but for all areas of HRM. It can be really helpful to reach out to a range of organizations to explore what they do and consider what elements of their approach might, or might not, have value in your organization. This may sound time-consuming (which to a degree it is) and you may have a good idea as to what would work and align to your organization; however, it is important to fully consider a range of options before coming to any conclusion. As well as face-to-face networking there are many useful forums on social media where you can seek out opinion from other HR professionals.

Also consider what, if any, published research exists to support a particular approach. For example, Journals such as the *Harvard Business Review* contain really accessible research in HRM and wider business areas. Increasingly we speak of the importance of evidence-based HR, so seeking out evidence to support the approach you are taking alongside shaping the solution to suit the needs and context of your organization is a powerful combination. It will also support any business case you need to present to senior leaders to get their buy-in and will strengthen credibility.

Working with stakeholders

From the point of analysis and planning through to implementation it is important that there is stakeholder involvement. First, it is important to understand who the stakeholders are. The stakeholders in performance management are those individuals, groups or organizations that either have an interest in, provide input into, or will be affected in some way by performance management, directly or indirectly. Taking this definition as guidance, stakeholders in the performance process are likely to include senior management, line management and employees. However, they may also include unions and employee representative bodies. Stakeholders may also be external to the organization, such as government bodies, clients or customers. It can sometimes be helpful to separate stakeholders into two categories: those with an immediate, close interest in performance management and those who may have an indirect, limited involvement. There are a variety of stakeholder mapping or analysis tools. Many use the two axes of the degree of interest the individual has in the project, and of the degree of power or influence the individual can yield in the organization. Typically, those most interested and most powerful will require considerable focus, communication and engagement to support successful outcomes. This separation can then help in ensuring that communication and activities during development and implementation are targeted and managed appropriately.

Once stakeholders are identified, the next stage will be to understand their particular interest, required input and attitude towards the process. Different stakeholder groups may vary in terms of their attitude towards performance management and in the expectations they have of what they want a performance management process to do and to deliver in terms of output. For example, it may be that senior management see it as a method of aligning employee performance to the wider objectives of the organization; line managers may see it as a method of raising the performance of their teams; employees may see it as a way to gain development and career progression. Understanding these varied expectations and managing those expectations is an important aspect of the planning and analysis stage.

Activity

- Identify the stakeholders in the performance management process, both within and outside of your organization.

- Identify these stakeholders' interests, required input or involvement and likely attitudes towards/expectations of the performance management process.

- Separate the stakeholders into two groups: those with an immediate close interest in performance management and those with a more indirect, limited involvement.

- What challenges might these stakeholder interests present to your organization when introducing a new or revised performance management process?

- How might these challenges be managed or overcome?

Business rationale and identification of objectives

Once the context in which performance management is to be conducted is fully understood, it is important to establish a business rationale for any process that is to be implemented. As part of that process, it is important to identify the overall aims and objectives of the performance management process. It is crucial at this stage to have a clear sense of what senior management want from the process: what they have identified as the valuable output of the process. Not only does there need to be clear identification of the business rationale, but this needs to be strongly and visibly supported by the senior management team.

Part of the development of the business rationale and aims needs to involve some kind of cost/benefit analysis. Senior management may have a particular idea of what they want the performance management process to achieve, but they need to fully understand the implications in terms of required resources (for example, time and money) and this understanding may lead to a rethink in terms of what can realistically be achieved.

Writing in the context of learning and development Rosemary Harrison (2009) has stressed the importance of integrating the stages of planning and evaluation, a process that is also relevant for performance management. The establishment of clear criteria by which performance management can be evaluated needs to happen at the start of the planning process. A clear vision of what successful performance management should look like and deliver should provide a clear focus and understanding for all stakeholders; it is also important in terms of managing expectations in terms of what performance management can and should deliver (Chapter 8 explores in more depth the process of evaluating performance management).

Development: design

A strong understanding of context should shape what follows in terms of the design of the performance management process and its content.

Process

There are various considerations in terms of the process. First, it is necessary to define responsibilities within the performance management process. It is important here that HR is seen as an enabler and/or expert, rather than leading the process. Line managers, as has already been discussed, need to own and lead the process. Accordingly, it is important that roles and responsibilities are clearly defined, so that everyone involved understands what their contribution should be.

Agreed timings for activities are also important, both in terms of the frequency of activities such as the formal performance review, but also identifying the point during the year in which key activities will take place. For example, some organizations choose to conduct performance reviews on the year anniversaries of someone joining the organization, thus fitting in with the individual's timeline with the organization. Others choose a time in the year when all employees will have appraisals completed and this may lead into annual pay reviews. There are no rights or wrongs here: it depends on what is right for the organization. If all reviews are to happen at the same time, a realistic time needs to be allocated for completion, particularly in the situation where the manager has a wide span of control (as discussed above).

It is also important that any process allows sufficient time for gathering of data and feedback for the performance review. For example, any process that incorporates the gathering of 360-degree feedback is likely to take considerably longer than a process that just involves feedback from the appraiser and upward feedback from the appraisee.

Content and documentation

The degree to which there should be a standardized approach to documentation will depend on the organization. The complexity of the data required to support any process will clearly impact on the nature of the documentation. For example, where there is a heavy reliance on collecting behavioural data, as well as data related to specific goals, the documentation is likely to be lengthier in nature.

One of the major criticisms of performance management processes over the years has related to the amount of bureaucracy involved, in particular the depth/breadth of form-filling that has been required. Technology has eased the burden somewhat, but the volume of documentation requiring completion still appears to be an area of concern in many organizations.

A balance needs to be struck between the need to capture the required data to support the objectives of performance management and the time required of individuals to complete the documentation. The type of organization and its culture will impact on choices made with regard to documentation. Some organizations that are naturally fairly bureaucratic in nature may feel it is entirely appropriate to have fairly lengthy detailed documentation supporting performance management. Many public sector organizations have fairly lengthy form-filling as part of their appraisal process, although there has been a growing shift away from this in recent years. For other organizations, significant documentation may cause frustration for employees, such as those working in the creative industries for example. Whatever documentation is to be used, the key factor is that individuals should be able to see the point and value of that documentation.

The presentation of any documentation should be supportive of the objectives of performance management. For example, when requiring a significant amount of qualitative feedback it is important to allow space for that feedback. However, forms that allow far too much space can be intimidating, particularly for the appraisee required to self-assess. Documentation that is not 'fit for purpose' causes frustration for users and will impact on the quality of data captured, so it is important that careful thought goes into the design process.

Technology

Both in terms of content and process design, technology is likely to have a vital place in supporting performance management. It is important that the information technology (IT) infrastructure, both in terms of any HR system but also in terms of integration with payroll and finance systems, is fully understood. There is no point designing a process only to find that the data capture or workflow route cannot be supported through the IT infrastructure. In terms of the stakeholder involvement mentioned above, the IT department has a key role to play in terms of input into practicality of the design of any process. Functionality can be explored and potential problems identified early on, reducing delay and costs later in the process.

Over the years I have worked with a variety of human resource information systems (HRIS), both at selection and implementation stages and as a day-to-day user. My experiences of HRIS have been mixed, but I have learnt some important lessons regarding their use:

- The most important lesson is that HR systems should be led by HR to support organizationally aligned HR objectives rather than be led by the IT department.

- Where there is the opportunity to bring in a new HRIS it is important to stay focused on the HR processes and objectives it is designed to support. (I have sat through many sales presentations for HRIS and have been blinded with the breadth of functionality – and it is easy to lose sight of the core functionality required.)

- An HRIS is only as good as the data it contains.

- If an organization is not using the data on an HRIS and there is not a reason (such as a legal requirement) for it being held, the organization should question whether it needs to continue to hold and capture that data. Significant costs are associated with the capturing of data so consideration of cost/benefit is important here.

- As with all areas of HR activity, the usage of HRIS needs to be regularly reviewed and evaluated. It may be that the collection of data previously identified as important no longer has relevance and, therefore, costs can be saved by no longer collecting, storing and processing that data.

- All users needed to be trained. This is particularly relevant now in the days of e-HR with line managers and employees having increasing involvement with both inputting and accessing data within the HRIS. If organizations want to empower managers and employees to be active participants in HRIS, then they need to be provided with the knowledge, skill and confidence to do so.

- If the trend continues to a shift away from annual appraisals to more regular check-in, some careful thought needs to be given as to how performance data will be captured, how often and by whom. HR analytics is an important area for the profession and the world of work moving forward. Organizations and HR need to consider what types of data are needed to drive performance moving forward. More frequent performance conversations will surely add value, but we also need to think about how we will capture performance data at an individual level to build a wider picture of trends in performance across the organization.

Activity

- What does your organization use in terms of an HRIS?

- Who has access to the data on the HRIS (HR, line managers, senior management, employees)?

- Who inputs data onto the HRIS?

- Who would you say 'owns' the HRIS?

- How does the HRIS integrate with other IT systems in your organization such as payroll or finance?

- What contribution does the HRIS make to performance management in your organization? What data is captured and how is that data used?

- How do you think the HRIS could be used more effectively to support effective performance management in your organization? Draw up an action plan to support your ideas.

Implementation

Implementation of performance management, as with other process implementation, requires effective project management. In this section we will consider some of the key project management considerations for implementing a performance management process.

Project management

A range of tools can be used to support project management, but the most common are that of the Gantt chart or critical path analysis (CPA). Both of these tools graphically present the timeline of a project. A Gantt chart will plot the key activities of a project (when they commence and when they should be completed) within the entire project time frame. The chart will often also indicate responsibilities for the activities and create a visual representation of the flow of activities from project commencement to end. They can highlight where projects grow in complexity and workload, by highlighting when there are peaks of activity and use of resources.

The critical path analysis (CPA) is similar to a Gantt but more analytical in nature. It will show the order and dependencies of tasks, highlighting where one task cannot take place without successful completion of another.

Typical stages of a project are the conception, development and implementation. So far we have explored the conception and development phases and we will now look in depth at the implementation stage. At this point the following should have been achieved:

- clear definition of aims and objectives;
- identification of resource requirements;
- identification of stakeholders and stakeholder interest;
- agreed process and documentation;
- identification of technology requirements to support process;
- outline of deliverables (against which evaluation will take place).

The project team

It is important that the project team is chosen carefully to include the key people required to implement the project effectively. Key considerations here are technical capability, for example a representative from IT is likely to be important; and knowledge and some of the 'softer skills' such as influencing. Diversity in the team is important to ensure a range of capability is included and also a range of viewpoints to avoid the dangers of 'group think'.

Once the team is identified it is important that the team leader ensures strong, open communication between team members and aims to create an environment where that team is motivated to perform. Clear goals, regular feedback including support and encouragement when the project encounters set backs, and celebration of success such as hitting milestones are all important here.

Milestones and control

Monitoring and controlling a project is key to delivering a project on time and ensuring resources are used effectively and appropriately throughout. Tools such as the Gantt can be used here to support monitoring and controlling. For example, it is helpful to identify key milestones in the project. Milestones provide points of review during the project, when it is expected that certain things will have been achieved. If the milestone has been hit then it is likely that the project will continue as originally planned; however, if a problem is identified then a process of analysis, problem solving and planning may need to take place in order to get the project back on track and to deliver within the time frame. It is sensible at the outset to build in some contingency time for things that may not go exactly to plan.

It is not only time that needs to be monitored and controlled: other resources such as costs also need to be monitored and reviewed. A performance management process that is implemented on time, but exceeds the budget allocated, may not offer the cost/benefit previously identified and is also likely to incur the wrath of the financial director. The process should have had carefully budgeted costings and it is important that they are not allowed to spiral upwards due to the absence of monitoring and control mechanisms.

Piloting

Running a pilot of the performance management process before an organization-wide roll-out is an invaluable tool in the implementation process. In larger organizations in particular, where there may be considerable diversity in terms of functional areas and job roles, it is worth pilot-testing performance management in two or three different areas. What may work well in your organization's finance team, for example, may be problematic for the marketing team. Identifying problems early on can save time and money in the long term.

Pilot testing also highlights the level of knowledge and skills of participants in the process. It may, for example, identify an area where employees may require more support in being active participants in giving upward feedback to their managers during their appraisal; suitable learning and development interventions can then be identified to close this learning gap. During pilot stages, employees can be identified who can help support and drive performance management implementation across the organization by acting as trainers, coaches or change agents, promoting their own positive experiences with the process and communicating the benefits to others in the organization. It is helpful to be aware of the key 'influencers' in the organization (as discussed at the start of this chapter) and where possible involve them in any pilot test that takes place.

Communication and engagement

An important part of the implementation process is a clear communication and engagement plan. This should be integrated with the overall project plan and link into the key milestones of the project. There should be regular, transparent communication and that communication should be two-way. Stakeholders should be provided with as close to real-time information on key developments as possible and be empowered to provide feedback and feel that their feedback is being listened to. As with any change programme there are dangers that where formal channels of communication fail, informal channels/rumours can take control, leading to misunderstanding and potentially impacted on project outcomes.

There are a range of communication activities that can be considered here:

- *Regular updates on progress from the project team.* These can be electronically via e-mail or intranet, or face-to-face depending on the organization context. The objective here is ensuring that everyone is updated with consistent messaging about the project and can reflect on what that means for them. Communicating success stories is important here so people can see that progress is being made towards the project goals.

- *Surveys.* Taking the temperature of feeling within the organization as the project rolls out can be helpful in identifying problems/issues swiftly and enabling action to deal with them to take place. It is also important in demonstrating that people have a voice in the change that is happening. Pulse surveys on the intranet are quick and effective in doing this.

- *Focus groups.* These can be helpful where a particular issue or problem has come up and where the project team needs to explore this in depth with questioning and debate to draw out views. Maybe there has been a resistance to introducing 360-degree feedback into the organization. A focus group might draw out some themes as to why and unearth ways to move forward. Alternatively, a series of semi-structured interviews could serve the same purpose if it is difficult to get groups of people together at the same time.

- *Formal organization channels.* Where organizations have recognized trade unions, work councils, Joint Consultative Committees, etc, it is obviously important that these forums are embedded into your communication plans. Their support and engagement will provide strong support behind any change.

Activity

Consider the communication channels and forums in your own organization:

- Which will you need to ensure are part of your communication plans?

- What key methods can you currently use to ensure effective communication and engagement?

- Do you have sufficient channels for upward and downward communication?

- What channels or forums might you need to introduce to support your project plan?

Training

The approach taken to training users of the performance management process will very much depend on the complexity of the process itself, the organizational context and particularly the resources available to the organization for training provision. It will also be dependent on the existing knowledge and skill set of the users of the process. In my experience there are a few key points that need to be considered when supporting performance management with training interventions:

- There is little doubt that where support isn't provided through some form of training intervention, users of the performance management process may lack the skills and/or confidence to participate effectively and this will impact on the overall success of the process. Knowledge, attitude and skill set among users are all important factors here.

- Both appraiser and appraisee need to be provided with the skills, knowledge and confidence to participate in the process. Also those required to deliver feedback need to have the skills, knowledge and confidence to participate effectively.

- If managers are taken out of their day-to-day jobs to attend a training course in performance management, such as handling performance reviews, you need to ensure the following:

  - They can see a clear purpose to the training, with the learning objectives clearly identified and value explained.

  - Whoever is facilitating the training has a general understanding of the operational issues the managers face as well as having expertise in the content of the training. The facilitator must be seen as credible, an expert in their field, but also someone who can relate good practice to the particular circumstances and challenges of the organization and context that the particular employee is working in.

  - The sessions should be highly participatory. Sitting listening to a lecture or watching a video on effective performance management is a poor substitute for exercises that involve applying learning. Exercises that enable the delegates to use active listening, or to role-play constructive feedback can be particularly powerful learning aids. Quite often managers are able to explain how to give constructive feedback, but when placed in a role-play situation may find the process much harder. This enables them to identify areas they need to work on in terms of their own development.

- It is not a great idea to have a manager attend the same course as their direct reports, as both parties may feel uncomfortable and the reporting line may inhibit them from being open in terms of any elements being taught that may cause them concern, or from contributing personal examples to the discussions.

- It is important that managers leave with a clear idea of what they will do differently as a result of the training intervention: a clear plan of action in terms of how to apply the learning they have gained.

- Follow-up to any training intervention is very important. In my experience, some of the best people management skills development sessions for line managers involve a session of training (be it a morning, a whole day or longer), followed by a gap when line managers return to the workplace and apply the learning. There then should be a follow-up session, typically three months later, when managers can explore how they have been applying the learning. They should be encouraged to identify successes, things that have worked well and improved performance management, and also identify problems. These problems can be explored with the group and strategies identified to address them and to enable the manager to manage performance more effectively moving forward.

Many organizations I have encountered do appear to offer some form of training when a new performance management process is introduced, or when a significant change to the process takes place. However, there is often little follow-up in terms of learning and development as managers' experience with the process grows. There is also often little provision to provide training and support for new managers coming into the organization, or employees promoted into positions where they are required to performance manage others for the first time. It may be that where such needs exist there are not the numbers to justify a structured off-the-job approach to training, but there needs to be some kind of learning intervention to ensure that any gap is addressed in terms of the knowledge, skill or confidence of these managers. Induction might be an area where the gap could be addressed, but also coaching either by another line manager or HR might also be a potential solution to close the gap. Taylor (2008) writes: 'proper training can be highly effective in reducing the extent to which appraisers fall into the most common traps. It also appears to bring substantial improvements to the level of objectivity observed.'

CASE STUDY

Brad Taylor, FCIPD, is the CIPD's Director of People. Brad joined the CIPD in June 2016. He started his career with Barclays Plc, working across both HR and non-HR roles, before moving into the not-for-profit sector, where he was Director of HR & Workplace with CIMA.

One of the areas that the CIPD HR team reviewed in 2017 was that of performance management. Having listened to managers and people in the organization, the existing approach to objective setting and the annual appraisal was not delivering the added value and outcomes we knew it potentially could. It is a busy environment with an array of activities involved and therefore being joined up is important. People wanted timely feedback and reassurance that managers in different departments approached both the objective setting and review in a consistent way, whilst allowing for individual flexing of approach that worked for the different types of roles within the organization.

Recent research from the CIPD had found that development-focused conversations result in more reliable performance conversations. The CIPD wanted to apply this in our own organization, encouraging more use of development conversations, in particular focusing on what skills/capabilities will be learned during the life of the objective.

The legacy process of assigning performance grades was removed and the annual appraisal conversation replaced with monthly one-to-ones, where the focus is on progress against objectives, well-being and learning. To assist managers keeping a record of progress, a performance grid was introduced as a tool to track outcomes as well as attitude and behaviour. Rather than being a one-off rating tool, it is designed for managers to refer to as often as needed. Furthermore, the conversation was separated from pay review conversations to encourage more open and honest reflection.

Updating the process is one thing, but, in order to help people begin to make the transition, a series of workshops with line managers facilitated by members of the HR team were put in place. The focus was not just on explaining the process, but enabling discussion and exploration of ideas to take place.

To help provide focus and line-of-sight, individual performance plans were updated to include the organization's key (strategic) goals for the year. Heads of department then record their own area's objectives that will contribute to overall success so that their people can, in turn, draft their objectives that feed into the department's success. This alignment is really helpful in enabling individuals to understand how their performance impacts on the wider organization.

Understanding the result of these changes becomes apparent over time. Achievement of organizational goals is one important measure. Another is through monitoring regular pulse survey responses in associated areas such as satisfaction with line management and feeling able to contribute to the organization's success.

Moving forward, the CIPD is looking to automate the recording and tracking of these objectives in the future. The aim of this is for our leadership to better understand how resource is deployed: which activities are over-resourced/ under-resourced? Is resource spread too thinly across objectives? We intend to use the information gathered to enable more predictive people metrics and reporting, ie is the organization at risk of not achieving a goal or ahead of the curve?

Barriers to success

Over the years I have had the opportunity to identify – through feedback from students, HR professionals, line managers, senior managers and employees – some consistent themes in terms of the typical barriers to the successful implementation of performance management processes. These themes include:

- lack of visible commitment from senior management;

- poor resourcing;

- cynicism of employees due to negative previous experience;

- lack of required skill or knowledge of participants to carry out implementation.

A useful tool here is Lewin's Forcefield Analysis (1947), a method often used in analysing change. It involves:

- analysing the forces driving change (for example, the need for more effective management of performance, or senior management commitment);

  - ·sing the forces that may be restraining change (for example, lack of ·es, or employee attitudes);

    - · the strength of the driving and restraining forces (for example, whether these forces are high, medium or low in terms of their ·act on the process of change);

- taking action to support and enhance the high-driving forces and to decrease the potential impact of the high-restraining forces is likely to create a situation where change can be achieved.

The activity below is based on this technique.

Activity

Whether you are looking to introduce a completely new performance management process, or implement some changes to an existing process, there is a need for change. In order to achieve change consider the following:

- What factors are driving the need for change and supporting the process of change?

- What factors are restraining the achievement of change? What factors may form barriers against the successful implementation of a new or changed performance management process?

- Once you have identified the driving and restraining forces, sort them into three categories in terms of their likely impact on the process (high, medium, low).

- What can be done to maximize the impact of the driving forces?

- What can be done to minimize the impact of the restraining forces, or to remove the barriers to change moving forward?

Monitoring and evaluation

It is vital that during the implementation of performance management there is an ongoing monitoring and evaluation process (this process will be explored in detail in Chapter 8). The stages of designing, developing and implementing the performance management process have been presented here in a linear way, but the reality for many organizations is that there is likely to be a degree of overlap between stages and there also may be a requirement to stop at a stage and revisit earlier activity. For example, a pilot test may highlight a particular problem in the design of the appraisal form, so the design stage will need to be revisited with the involvement of relevant stakeholders. Ongoing monitoring and reviewing will support a responsive and agile approach to the implementation of any performance management process.

This chapter has explored the practical aspects of implementing a performance management process in an organization. It has highlighted the factors that need to be taken into consideration in the design, development and implementation of performance management and the importance of involving and gaining the commitment of stakeholders in the process. In the next chapter we look at some of the key activities of performance management, in particular the fundamental activities of objective-setting and feedback.

Planning and action

06

The performance agreement

Performance planning commences with an agreement between a manager and an individual about the performance required. Armstrong and Baron (2005: 24) state that 'performance agreements record the agreed direction and form the basis for measurement, feedback, assessment and development in the performance management process'. As such, it is a critical element in the performance management process and it is very important that there is clarity of understanding of this agreement between the employee and the manager. It should provide a clear focus in terms of what performance is expected and a sound basis on which to assess performance during an agreed period. The performance agreement should also help give a sense of priorities, key activities and behaviours likely to result in added value. In terms of a new employee or an employee moving into a new role, that agreement is often developed from the outline of the job requirements that have been identified through the job analysis process.

Job analysis

Job analysis forms a basis for the performance agreement. The process involves the formal analysis of a job to provide detailed information on the job, role or task to be performed. The first essential question to answer is: Why does this job exist? A brief outline as to why is important in order to establish a rationale for all that follows. The process of job analysis can be almost scientific in nature; it certainly should be undertaken methodically. It is vital that accurate data are captured to give a true understanding of the nature of the job. Strategies may include all, or some, of the following:

- observation (by independent assessor, HR or line manager);
- diaries (kept by job holder, for example);

- interviews (conducted with job holder, line manager, other members of the team);
- questionnaires (as per interviews).

As with gathering 360-degree feedback in the performance management process, it is helpful to get a 360-degree perspective on the job by gathering data from various sources. The perspective held by the job holder might vary from that of their line manager or other members of the team. Identifying discrepancies and working through these to ascertain the true nature of the role is an important part of the job analysis process.

The process of job analysis aims to identify both the 'what' of the job, the key activities or responsibilities that need to be undertaken, but also the 'how', the qualities, behaviours and competencies that are needed to carry out the job effectively. Traditionally the outputs of the job analysis process have been the job description and the person specification. The job description should provide a summary of the tasks that make up a job, identify reporting lines and areas of responsibility, including any budgets to be managed. A person specification should focus away from the job content onto the attributes of an individual who would be able to carry out the role effectively. Person specifications will usually include headings such as skills, education, qualifications, competencies, experience. It is also common practice to divide these sections into essential – sending a clear message to candidates about their suitability for the role; and desirable – providing helpful objective differentiating data to make a selection decision. A sample job description and person specification for an HR administrator can be found opposite.

Sample job description and person specification

Job description

Job title: HR Administrator
Grade: 3
Reports to: HR Manager
Job purpose: To provide administration support for the HR team

Key responsibilities

- Providing administrative support for the HR team. This will include creating, maintaining and updating spreadsheets; producing and checking paperwork for new starters; updating the HR database; tracking progress and producing reports.

- Providing administrative support for recruitment processes, including logging applications in the HR database recording all candidate details, CVs and tracking the key recruitment stages through to selection.

- Checking, logging and distributing e-mails from company inbox.

- Co-ordinating interview arrangements and dealing with correspondence to/from job applicants and/or recruitment agencies.

- Scheduling induction programmes for new starters.

- Recording and updating holiday and absence records on HR database.

- Administering training and development both internally and externally, including making course bookings and logging all training and formal development activity onto the HR database.

- Other administrative HR tasks to support the HR team as may arise from time to time.

Person specification

Qualifications/training

Essential: a good standard of education (eg five GCSEs or equivalent including Maths and English grades A–C).

Desirable: CIPD Level 3 qualification or at least currently working towards; European Computer Driving Licence (ECDL).

Experience/knowledge

Essential

- At least 12 months' experience of human resources/personnel administration.

- Demonstrable experience of producing accurate employment documentation.

- Demonstrable experience of using a human resources database.

- Knowledge of general office practices and procedures.

- Knowledge of IT systems, databases, spreadsheets, word and e-mail.

Desirable: Experience of extracting, collating and presenting statistical information.

Skills and competencies

Essential

- Strong administrative skills.
- Ability to provide advice on company policy: employment terms, conditions and practices.
- Ability to communicate effectively with internal and external contacts at all levels.
- Ability to work to deadlines and within defined quality standards.
- Ability to compose and produce standard letters and reports using IT applications (Word, Excel, Outlook).
- Ability to deal sensitively and appropriately with confidential information.
- Ability to undertake routine calculations.
- Ability to work well as part of a team.
- Integrity and respect for confidentiality.

Desirable

- Willingness to work flexibly and provide cover and support across the team.
- Ability to produce PowerPoint presentations (training will be provided if necessary).
- Understanding of and commitment to equality of opportunity.
- Excellent customer service skills.

There has been some criticism of job descriptions in recent years that stems from various standpoints. First, there is the argument that because we are working in an environment of rapid change, these documents become out of date almost as soon as they are agreed. Second, it is argued that there is a lack of flexibility in a 'set' job description. Some organizations aim to combat this by adding vague flexibility clauses into job descriptions such as the one in our example, 'other administrative duties that arise from time to time'. Having said that, the job description certainly isn't dead; it is still used extensively in recruitment and selection and in performance management. Ideally the job description should be reviewed regularly to ensure it offers a reasonable reflection of the current job.

Some organizations have chosen to reject traditional job descriptions in favour of accountability profiles. Job descriptions tend to focus on tasks, whilst accountability profiles focus more on deliverables or outputs. These give a sense of the outcomes likely when there is effective performance in the job. For example, for the HR administrator role outlined above, one of the key elements of the accountability profile might be the production of accurate monthly reports on staff absence using the HR database. There is a more natural flow into the performance management process with such a document. Maitland and Thomson in their book *Future Work* (2011) challenge many of the conventional attitudes about work. They argue for the need for organizations to have a much greater focus on results rather than specific tasks to be undertaken, and the need for placing much greater flexibility with the worker in terms of how those results are achieved. An accountability profile fits much more effectively than a traditional job description with this model of a performance agreement.

The content of the performance agreement

The performance agreement provides a framework for an employee's performance to be managed. The employee will agree with his or her manager what performance should be achieved and the performance will be outlined in terms of both results and behaviours. As discussed above, the job analysis process will have produced some valuable data that can be incorporated into the agreement. The nature of the agreement will vary according to the nature and needs of the organization and type of role; however, some key elements are likely to be included. First, an outline of key results areas. This may be outlined first as broad key results areas for the role, then broken down into more detailed SMART objectives for a given time frame. Second, key behavioural competencies for the role may be outlined (both objective setting and competencies are discussed in greater length further on in this chapter). There also may be an outline of the requirement to uphold key organization values such as demonstrating mutual respect and honesty in dealing with others.

Objective setting

For organizations to manage performance effectively, it is vital that everyone understands clearly what they are required to do to contribute to the success of the organization. Objective setting for individuals and teams is therefore a very important part of the performance management process.

The acronym SMART is often used to provide guidance in effective objective setting. There are varied versions of SMART, but the one I find most helpful is as follows:

S	Specific	(there is clarity in terms of exactly what should be achieved)
M	Measurable	(the outcome can be measured)
A	Agreed	(manager and employee agree the outcome to be achieved)
R	Relevant	(relevant to the organization, so there is a link to overall business goals, but also relevant to the individual: do they feel this is an objective over which they have some control, and ability to impact on?)
T	Timebound	(there is a clear time frame for achievement of outcome)

If objectives are not specific and there is a lack of clarity in terms of what should be achieved, there are various potential negative consequences. First, the employee may misunderstand what needs to be achieved and focus on the wrong things. Second, the lack of clarity may cause the employee to feel anxious and unsure how to progress. Third, a lack of clarity in any objectives set presents potential problems when it comes to assessing performance against those objectives. This latter point is also very relevant to the requirement for an objective to be measurable. Both manager and employee should be able to clearly articulate what a successful achievement of the objective will look like. What criteria will be used in measuring that achievement? Without clear measures and assessment criteria in place, once again any assessment of performance becomes problematic.

The importance of agreement in objective setting reflects an overall approach to performance management that reflects a desire for consensus, commitment and participation rather than an authoritarian, controlling approach. The argument here is that employees are more likely to deliver good performance when they believe in the objectives to achieve, feel with a reasonable amount of effort they are achievable and have had a say in their formulation. This links back to some of the motivation theory we explored in Chapter 2. An objective imposed on an individual may still be met, but possibly not to the same standard, or without evidence of the discretionary behaviour – the extra 10 per cent of effort – which is more likely when an individual is truly motivated to perform.

The issue of relevance has two strands, as indicated above. The first strand is the connection between individual objectives and the wider goals of the organization. As explored in Chapter 3, an essential part of effective performance management is the cascading down of goals from organization level to team and individual. Individual performance should be aligned to the wider goals of the organization to ensure individuals are focused on activities that add value and contribute to organization success. From the individual's perspective this alignment gives a sense of contribution and meaningfulness. Much of the research into effective job design has shown that individuals are more likely to perform well in a job where they can make a connection between their work and the wider goals of the organization. This also helps develop a feeling of organization citizenship, feeling part of an organization rather than just working for an organization.

The second strand is that an individual should feel that the objective set is relevant to them. The danger with focusing on corporate objectives is that a connection is lost with the role the individual is carrying out. It is important that the individual feels that they have some control of and influence on the achievement of the objective. If not, there is a danger that the individual will feel there is little point putting in any effort as the final result cannot be influenced by their performance. This has a strong resonance with Vroom's Expectancy Theory of Motivation. The individual should believe that, with a reasonable amount of effort on their part, the objective can be achieved.

In terms of the timebound element, I think there are few people who would argue that a deadline doesn't focus the mind! It is important that there is clarity between the manager and the individual in terms of when the objective needs to be achieved by. This provides the focus of a deadline, but also enables the individual to plan their workload effectively, identifying priorities. With long-term objectives it may be helpful, in line with the principles of effective project management, to break these down and identify key dated milestones to be reached on the journey to achieving the objective.

There are, however, other factors that also should be considered in the objective-setting process beyond SMART. One consideration not covered by SMART is the requirement for objectives to provide an element of challenge or stretch. Motivation theories such as Locke's Goal Theory (1968) argue that for goals to motivate towards high performance there needs to be an element of challenge. An element of challenge will mean that once a goal is achieved there is likely to be a greater sense of achievement, another potential motivator. This element of challenge in objectives is an interesting one, because individuals will have varying needs and levels of capability for challenge and achievement. Here the role of the line manager in understanding those they manage becomes critical. Recognizing ability and knowledge levels, and also confidence and desire for challenge, is important. Some individuals will be hungry – and ready in terms of ability and knowledge – for stretching, challenging goals. Others for reasons such as levels of confidence, skills and knowledge or attitude may require a different approach. It is important to balance the needs of the organization with the capability of the individual and, where there is a mismatch, identify support strategies to enable the individual to take on the more challenging objectives required. A recent report by the CIPD on Performance Management (CIPD, 2016a), suggests that goal setting in some cases shouldn't necessarily be specific and challenging in nature. Whilst SMART goals work well for many situations, this research concluded that in some cases it can detract from successful performance, for example in more complex work where actual direction evolves as learning is achieved and where there is low initial predictability in terms of outcomes. This makes me think of individuals working in the field of research or product innovation where SMART objectives could be hard to define, and wider aims might provide a better framework for performance. The CIPD research refers to 'do-your-best' outcome goals. It may also be that it is appropriate to set an individual a mix of SMART and 'do-your-best' objectives depending on the role context.

Developmental objectives

Many organizations are also ensuring that alongside performance objectives, all individuals are set one or two development objectives. These are focused purely on the individual's personal development. For our HR administrator in the job description above, examples of such objectives could be as follows: 1) to gain experience of the disciplinary process, by sitting in at least one disciplinary meeting taking notes and debriefing the HR manager (a suitable time frame should be agreed for the completion of this objective); 2) to have successfully completed the company Level 1 Competency Interviewing Skills course within the next six months.

Once again it is important that these objectives are agreed between the individual and the manager. It is important for the individual to see a purpose and value to the development objective so that they truly own the process and give the necessary commitment to the learning process. As with other objectives, individuals are more likely to perform where they see a valuable outcome to the achievement of the objective.

Competencies

I was first introduced to the concept of competencies by a consultant who had come over from the US head office of the company I was then working for, to help us implement a competency framework in the UK. He delivered a powerful presentation explaining the nature and value of competencies, which began with the engaging title, 'What are competencies and why should I care?' So, what are competencies and why should you care? Why are they important to the performance management process? If tasks are the 'what' of performance, competencies are the 'how'. If we purely look at an individual's performance in terms of tasks completed, or objectives achieved, we are not getting a full picture of how the individual is performing. One of the most-used definitions of competencies is that of Boyzatis (1982): 'an underlying characteristic of a person which results in effective or superior performance in a job'. Another key word here is 'behaviour': what behaviours do we observe in a person carrying out the job well, as opposed to someone underperforming in the role?

Common competencies used in organizations today include the following:

- leadership;
- teamworking;
- customer focus;
- problem solving;
- developing others;
- building relationships;
- communication.

If we take the example of 'building relationships' from the list, let us use that competency to explore the importance of competencies in a short business scenario.

Scenario

Sam is a sales executive for a very successful marketing company. He has been with the organization for two years and Amanda, his line manager, is about to conduct his annual appraisal. Sam has had some tough sales targets this year, particularly in the current climate. He has done really well hitting his targets, sometimes even ahead of the timescale set, and so he is heading into his appraisal confident that he will receive positive feedback. Amanda begins the appraisal by asking Sam how he feels he has done and he confidently explains he feels he has performed extremely well, achieved all the targets set and in some cases exceeding expectations. Amanda asks Sam whether there is anything about his performance he felt could have been improved, anything he could do better moving forward. Sam thinks for a minute and says, 'I think I could have pushed for better deals in some instances, I could negotiate harder. Also, I think I could get more out of my team, I sometimes feel I am carrying them rather than them supporting me.'

Amanda takes this opportunity to explore the areas of Sam's performance that are giving her concern. First, she has had some negative feedback from clients who have objected to Sam's rather aggressive sales style. An important element of negotiation in the workplace is the fact that relationships are of an ongoing nature, so both parties need to leave the negotiation process without too much of a sour aftertaste. There should be a willingness to do business together again. Sam might have achieved a good deal with some clients, but Amanda is concerned that the clients may not choose to work with the company again, or at least with Sam, if his aggressive approach continues.

The second area of concern is Sam's management of his team. In the two years that Sam has worked for the company, his team of three have all moved out of their roles. One of his team moved to another job in the company and the other two, even more worryingly, moved to another organization. One of the factors in the move for all three was Sam's coercive, pace-setting style of leadership. His team members gradually had become worn-down under this style, feeling they were given little support or understanding from Sam.

Sam's perspective is very black and white. He has been asked to achieve certain things by the organization and he has delivered, over-delivered in places and therefore cannot see any problem. If his staff can't take the pressure then he will get people in who can, and he is confident he can smooth over any ruffled feathers with clients. Amanda sees that if she is to change Sam's performance, she needs to change the nature of the performance agreement to focus not just on what Sam does but how he does it: in other words some behavioural, competency targets need to be put in place.

'Building relationships' could be an important competency here to help Sam achieve improved performance both for himself and the company. His current behaviour is very short-termist. It is unlikely that clients will continue to work with an executive with such an aggressive approach, which is a real concern for the organization. Sam has also wasted a lot of time interviewing and training new team members. He could save himself much time if he could improve the retention of his team. High staff-turnover is both costly and disruptive for organizations. Sam may well be right in his claim to be carrying the team. If they are demotivated by his leadership style, they may not be performing to their best ability and are highly unlikely to be demonstrating any discretionary behaviour. A more empowering, engaging leadership style would be more likely to get him the kind of support from his team that he needs. There is great value to be gained for both Sam and the organization if he can develop behaviours to sustain positive relationships both with clients and with his direct reports.

Michael Armstrong (2009) outlines a helpful performance management matrix that was developed by Ann Cummins of Humanus Consultancy for a client in the financial services sector (see Figure 6.1). It provides us with an effective visual way of plotting an individual's performance, taking into consideration both what they do and how they do it. It provides us with ways of looking at an individual's performance holistically, in terms of results delivered, or outputs, but also the inputs – behaviours, attitudes and overall approach.

Looking at the performance matrix, our ideal is to have all our employees working well within the top-right quadrant. If we consider Sam, the sales executive from our scenario, we would expect to see him plotted in the top-left quadrant. He is a high achiever in terms of output; however, there are some significant concerns in relation to behaviours, attitude and overall approach to work. Individuals in this quadrant will need support,

FIGURE 6.1   Performance matrix

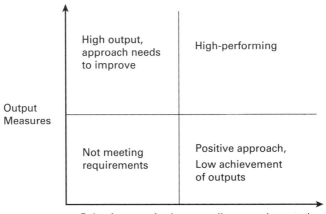

SOURCE Armstrong (2009)

through interventions such as coaching, in order to be able to demonstrate new behaviours. In my experience this is one of the hardest areas to work on in terms of changing performance. It is not as straightforward as working with an individual to improve the knowledge or skill set required to deliver objectives (as might be considered for individuals in the bottom-right quadrant). Individuals in the top-left quadrant may need to change their attitudes about the way a job should be carried out, the way they need to behave. This also sometimes requires the individual to accept that others perceive their behaviours differently to how they see themselves in the workplace. For example, an individual may feel they are just being assertive at work, whilst others perceive this behaviour as aggressive, even bullying. Here, 360-degree feedback can be helpful (as explored later in this chapter); it is harder to argue against feedback from a range of people as opposed to the direct feedback from one, usually your line manager.

Activity

Using a few blank copies of the performance matrix, consider two or three individuals you are working with at the current time. If you were to plot them on the grid, where would they be? Mark them with an X and then consider what possible action steps you could take to manage their performance moving forward. We will revisit this matrix when we look at underperformance in Chapter 7, but start thinking about strategies you might be able to use to support effective performance.

Don't forget the individuals performing in the upper-right quadrant: there is a danger of overlooking them and focusing on bringing up your underperformers. The individuals in this quadrant need to be sure they are on your radar and that they are being recognized and rewarded for delivering the performance you require. They will also need to be stretched and challenged to maintain levels of motivation and avoid drifting into complacency.

Developing a competency framework

There are a variety of ways to develop a competency framework and, of course, competencies will be embedded in your organization's recruitment and selection as well as performance management processes. Some organizations will look to identify core competencies to cover all the

TABLE 6.1 Levels within a competency

Teamworking
Level 1
Listens to others and considers their views.
Shares learning and information openly with others.
Handles disagreement constructively, seeking positive solutions.
Level 2
Works towards better understanding of others, their abilities and needs.
Encourages involvement of others and offers to share experiences and knowledge with others.
Recognizes sensitive situations and identifies ways of managing them.
Level 3
Effectively brings the skills and knowledge of others together to achieve team goals.
Actively works to ensure all members of the team are able to make an effective contribution and supports others through coaching.
Demonstrates high levels of emotional intelligence in interactions with others, understanding self and others to maintain effective working relationships.

roles in the organization; others will look to establish frameworks for specific areas or levels. Much will depend on the complexity, structure and culture of the organization. Where a framework covers a wide range of roles with different demands, the behavioural indicators within each competency may be divided into a series of levels. An example is provided in Table 6.1.

Some competency frameworks also provide contra-indicators, that is behaviours that work in direct opposition to fulfilment of a particular competency. In relation to teamworking it could be: withholding relevant information, knowledge or experiences from others. Sometimes, of course, it is easier to help an individual understand what is required in a role by providing examples of things to avoid doing.

There are many competency frameworks readily available through professional bodies such as those that form part of the CIPD's Profession Map. These are clearly a helpful starting point for specific professional areas. However, many organizations wanting a wider competency framework will need to take time and a structured approach to developing a relevant framework that has the support of the people in the organization. Developing a competency framework will involve a detailed data-gathering process, which is usually targeted around gaining information such as the following at organization level:

- What behaviours are currently driving success in our organization?
- What behaviours are currently impeding success?
- What behaviours will be important for success in the future?

Then, looking specifically at the role level:

- How do our high performers behave when they are carrying out their roles?
- What is it that differentiates our high performers from our average performers?

There are a variety of ways to gather data. Typical methods will be:

- Use of existing data (such as that provided by professional bodies).
- Internal focus groups or workshops, where a group of people who have 'expert' knowledge or experience of the job – managers and job holders – work with a facilitator to identify effective and less effective behaviours, recorded on flip charts.
- Structured interviews, where detailed exploration takes place of how people carry out their jobs. This aims to identify what differentiates the behaviour of an organization's superior performers from its average performers.
- Critical incident techniques, which focus not on the entirety of a role but a specific critical moment in carrying out the role where it is essential that superior performance is demonstrated. A typical example of this would be when dealing with a customer complaint.

Developing a competency framework takes time and expertise. Structured, behavioural interviewing is not easy and individuals will need to be trained to conduct interviews effectively in order to draw out the necessary level of detail to capture the data required to build a framework. For this reason, organizations may choose to bring in external consultants with the expertise and objectivity required. Once a competency framework is in place it can then provide a valuable tool to help ensure the right people are recruited and selected into the organization and that once in, their performance is managed effectively. Individuals are not just assessed on what they do, but the behaviours that the organization knows can make a difference between average performers and a superior performance, which enables the organization to achieve its goals.

Criticisms of competency frameworks

We shouldn't move on from any discussion on competencies without considering the criticisms that have been levelled at the use of competencies in organizations. Many organizations have spent much time and money producing complex competency frameworks, supported by glossy brochures and lengthy training sessions, only to see them slowly disappear under a carpet of dust as time moves on. Typical criticisms focus on the amount of time and bureaucracy involved in their use and a lack of relevance to the roles carried out. Competency frameworks can sometimes use language that is unnecessarily confusing and complex. There are also inherent challenges in gathering objective data on behaviours.

There are no simple answers to these problems; however, there are some key action steps that organizations can take to improve the likelihood of successful implementation and the ongoing success of a competency framework:

- Involvement of key stakeholders in the development of the framework.

- Sufficient time, resources and expertise provided.

- Training and support for users. Managers will need support just as in other areas of performance management. The ability to give feedback (as explored later in this chapter) is particularly important. Individuals themselves, if required to self-assess, will need support in being able to identify specific examples of the behaviours looked for.

- Remember that the focus is on the end of delivering high performance, and don't allow this to be lost sight of in unnecessarily complex processes and language. Simplicity and relevance are important factors.

Core values

Increasingly organizations have also incorporated a commitment to and demonstration of core values as part of the performance agreement. Core values define the character and ideology of an organization. They provide guidance in terms of how the organization and the people working for the organization will conduct themselves both internally and with the external world. Expectations of individual behaviour can be linked to these core values in the performance agreement. Values will, of course, vary according to the organization, but common ones include:

- quality;
- continuous improvement;
- innovation;
- integrity;
- mutual respect.

In recent years, there has been recognition of the need to demonstrate a commitment to ethical behaviour and this is often reflected in the core values of an organization. Words such as respect, honesty, responsibility and transparency are all likely to appear within core values.

CASE STUDY

Writing in the *Guardian* in February 2013, Helen Crane reported that a new competency framework was being introduced into the civil service. These competencies would be incorporated into the performance management process and were designed with the aim of developing a greater commercial focus within the organization and to break down silos between sections of the civil service: 'The new competency framework will also make it easier for civil servants to apply for jobs in other departments and for managers to identify areas for improvement.'

I was interested in the report and explored the new competency framework further. Behaviours appear to have been placed at the heart of performance management and are designed to support the civil service values of honesty, integrity, impartiality and objectivity. The framework outlines 10 competencies, grouped into three clusters: setting direction, engaging people and delivering results. There are levels within each competency linking to seniority of roles, and indicators of behaviours are provided with the aim of both helping understanding of what is required and of ensuring consistency in terms of performance expectations. As well as providing indicators of effective performance, examples of ineffective performance are provided. In my experience this can be particularly useful in helping employees to understand the types of behaviour that should be avoided and that impede the delivery of effective performance in their jobs. Below are two examples taken from the framework.

Under the strategic cluster – setting direction, one of the competencies is 'Seeing the Big Picture'. At Level 6 (Director General and Director) an example of effective behaviour is given as: *understand where the department sits within and aligns across the civil service*; and an example of ineffective behaviour as: *focus on own immediate area of concern and not see interconnections across the civil service*. This would appear to link well into the organization's objective of breaking down silos.

Under the strategic cluster – delivering results, one of the competencies is 'Achieving Commercial Outcomes'. At Level 4 (Grade 7 and 6 or equivalent) an example of effective behaviour is given as: *understand the commercial drivers that will influence a private or third sector organization and the levers that can be used in negotiating/influencing contractual arrangements*; and an example of ineffective behaviour as: *show little or no understanding or appreciation of the economic drivers that will influence the behaviour of suppliers*. This would appear to link well into the organization's objective of developing a greater commercial focus.

There is a clear recognition here that performance is not just about the tasks people carry out, but the way in which they behave in carrying out those roles. This framework also demonstrates how competencies can be used to align performance to organizational goals and the core values of the organization.

Full details of the new competency framework can be found on the civil service website (**www.civilservice.gov.uk**) if you would like to explore this further.

Feedback

An essential part of the performance management process is giving people feedback on how they are doing. Well before entering the world of work, we seek feedback from others – our parents, teachers and friends – to gain a sense of how we are doing. Feedback that is well delivered can help us move on from mistakes, can help us identify areas to develop, or provide reassurance and build confidence. Feedback poorly delivered can leave us confused, worried, angry or demotivated. It is important that organizations provide an environment where feedback is used constructively to encourage the performance required. Feedback should provide us with information about our performance in terms of our behaviours (inputs) and performance outcomes. It should also provide us with timely information relating to critical incidents, such as a mistake. Feedback should enable us to gain an enriched understanding of how we are performing and what we need in order to improve or develop our performance moving forward. We can only take positive action when we have an appropriate understanding of what is required and how we are doing against that requirement.

Two-way and continuous feedback

We have thankfully moved on from the days when at the end of a shift an employee's supervisor would place a marker beside the individual and the colour of that marker would indicate whether the worker's performance had been good, acceptable or poor. Feedback has become more sophisticated and, in particular, is no longer totally focused on top-down feedback from manager to worker. There is a recognition now of the need for a more discursive approach to feedback and the benefit of upward feedback from employee to manager. Both parties can benefit from honest and objective feedback about how things are going. A two-way exchange of information has an important role in building positive working relationships and maintaining the all-important trust between employee and manager.

Just as performance management is an ongoing continuous process, so feedback should be an ongoing continuous process. Problems arise when feedback is withheld until the annual appraisal, for example. Long gaps should not be left between a particular performance moment and the giving of feedback. Time lapse often results in a lack of clarity of facts and makes it more difficult to draw effective conclusions and learning from a particular situation. Feedback should therefore be timely in order to have a positive impact on performance moving forward.

A balance needs to be struck between suffocating an individual with constant commentary on how they are doing and providing them with enough feedback for them to feel reassured and rewarded for performance, or to have enough information to change the nature of their performance if required. This requires the manager to take time to understand the individual they are managing: to recognize the employee's levels of skill, knowledge and confidence in relation to the job, and also their particular personality type. Some individuals need more reassurance, while others will be happy to work with less. There will also be some employees who feel they don't need feedback, yet it is important that they not only hear that feedback, but take it on board moving forward. The most successful managers are those who can adapt their approach to the needs of an individual to ensure that feedback is given in a timely way, when needed by the individual and the organization in order to achieve the best results.

Constructive feedback

When handled badly, feedback can result in decreased performance. When feedback is delivered in a negative manner, employees are likely to become demotivated and unlikely to improve their performance. Feedback should be about providing information to enable improved performance, rather than a judgemental approach. It is important that feedback is given in such a way that doesn't damage an individual's self-esteem; rather they should feel motivated and able to change things moving forward.

Constructive feedback provides factual information. Statements from a manager that begin 'I feel' or 'I think' immediately sound subjective. Compare these two statements: 1) 'I don't think you are very good at dealing with customer complaints'; 2) 'When you dealt with that last customer complaint, I observed that you raised your voice and were not actively listening to the customer's concerns.'

The first statement is an opinion and does not provide any specific examples. It is also judgemental and focused on the individual rather than the task they are carrying out. If you were receiving this feedback think about which of those two statements is more likely to equip you with knowledge to improve your performance. In the first statement, clearly more information is needed and support required for the employee to improve performance moving forward; the second statement provides the employee with a specific example of behaviours that are working against the achievement of good performance. The manager in this situation could follow on from point two with the next statement: 'The next time you deal with a customer complaint, aim to keep your voice calm and reflect back what the customer is saying in order to show you are listening and have understood and then provide the appropriate response to their complaint.'

A final point about constructive feedback is to focus on key elements of an individual's performance. If you present them with a huge list of things to improve/do differently, they are likely to feel overwhelmed and demotivated and unable to take the feedback and move forward effectively. In most cases, there are two or three things individuals could do differently at work that will make a considerable difference to their performance. Focus on these. The desire for meaningful feedback is highlighted by a recent CIPD report (CIPD, 2016a). It is the quality of the feedback that will determine successful performance outcomes. Interestingly, and also reassuringly in these days of flexible working, this research also highlighted that the medium of that feedback appears to be unimportant (whether e-mail, Skype, face to face, etc). What is important is that the feedback is convincing and is an enabler for the individual to move forward positively in terms of their performance as a result.

360-degree feedback

As discussed earlier, we have seen a shift away from the concept of purely top-down feedback in the performance management process. Initially, the main source of other feedback was that of upward feedback from employee to manager, but in more recent times much wider sources of feedback are sought in the performance management process.

The term 360-degree, in feedback terms, means feedback from a variety of sources that all may have a slightly different perspective or experience of an individual's performance. In today's working environment with complex working patterns and arrangements, it may well be that a line manager may have little day-to-day contact with an employee, they may well be working in a different country or even on a different continent to the employer. In order to give constructive, objective feedback for an individual, information needs to be drawn from those sources best able to provide a relevant perspective on an individual's performance. The benefit of 360-degree feedback is that it is valuable both to the individual and the organization as it provides multiple perspectives on an employee, providing a more holistic understanding of how the individual is performing. It can be particularly helpful when assessing competencies in performance management. While data-gathering in terms of objectives achieved can often be quite straightforward for a line manager looking at outcomes, behaviours need to be observed by people working alongside an individual. When there is consistency across feedback received that certain behaviours need to be developed or changed to improve performance, this can be a much stronger catalyst to change for the employee than feedback from just one source.

Sources of 360-degree feedback – as well as from the manager and employee – may include peers, direct reports and even customers and clients. Indeed, back in 2010 *People Management* magazine reported that Cadbury were introducing '720-degree feedback' as part of a new leadership development programme. This feedback was to include input from a leader's friends and family, as well as business colleagues and direct reports – a thought that I have to say fills me with some horror!

In the 1990s 360-degree feedback became somewhat of a fad, with many organizations jumping on the bandwagon with little thought to the purpose of the feedback or the value. Many initiatives ended in failure, because there had not been a clear strategy in place for implementation. Many companies drowned in the bureaucracy and time required to gather and collate feedback and, in some cases, poorly trained managers were ill-equipped to collate and deliver feedback. However, many organizations today do use 360-degree feedback effectively in a way that adds value to the performance management process. Below are some considerations for its implementation.

Implementing 360-degree feedback

First, an organization should be very clear on why they wish to implement 360-degree feedback and identify what outcomes they expect to see if the process is working effectively. If no valuable outcomes can be identified, my response would be 'why do it?' It takes time and commitment to implement and manage this feedback effectively, so there should be some clear valuable outcomes.

An appropriate organization culture and employee-relations backdrop is needed to support 360-degree feedback. High levels of trust, and a culture of open, honest communication will support its implementation; a blame culture where everyone is watching their back will not. Usually feedback is given anonymously in order to encourage openness and honesty; however, without a supportive organization backdrop, individuals may still feel anxious about giving honest feedback and instead only offer benign commentary. The organization must be ready for 360-degree feedback and the senior management team must be willing to give the process their active commitment.

Implementation can be as simple or as complex as suits the needs of your organization. One of the most powerful tools I ever used in terms of 360-degree feedback was the simple 'start, stop and continue' tool. A variety of sources are asked to complete a simple sheet, which asks the person giving feedback to identify three things an individual should start doing to improve their performance, three things a person should stop doing and three things a person should continue doing. Where consistent themes emerge, gaining an individual's acceptance of behavioural change should be easier to achieve.

Much more complex 360-degree tools may be used, with detailed commentary against specific behavioural competencies. It is vital that sufficient resources are allocated to whatever process is decided on, both in terms of its design and implementation. Are adequate resources available in terms of employee time and budgets? Given the fact that many processes are now managed online, does the organization have the technology to support the process? Can it ensure there are sufficient resources for support and training for users?

Involve key stakeholders in the implementation process and gain ownership early on by involving employees at different levels in the organization. Ideally run a pilot test of any process in order to iron out any obvious issues before rolling out to the wider organization. Ensure mechanisms are in place to monitor and evaluate implementation (evaluation of performance management is explored in greater detail in Chapter 8).

Feedback and the Johari Window

The Johari Window (see Figure 6.2) is helpful in understanding the value of feedback. Developed by Luft and Ingham in 1955 it has been used in various formats to raise awareness in human behaviour and improve interrelations.

FIGURE 6.2   Johari Window

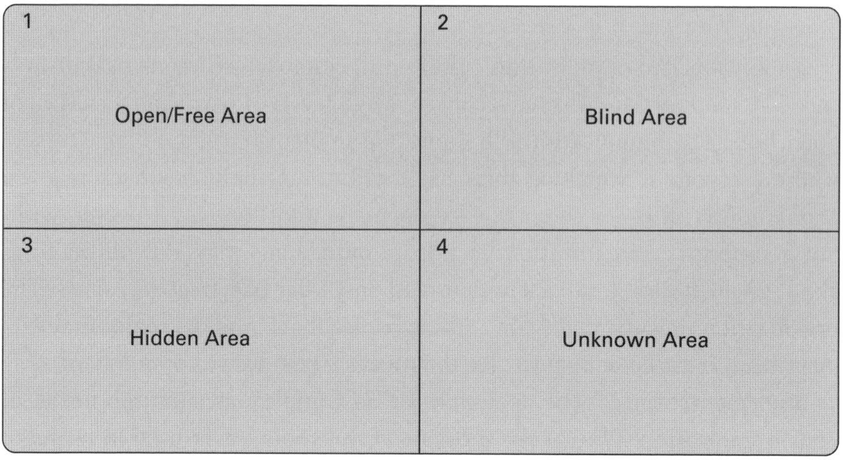

1	2
Open/Free Area	Blind Area
3	**4**
Hidden Area	Unknown Area

SOURCE Luft and Ingham

The four quadrants represent factors that are known to oneself and factors that are known to others. So in quadrant 1, the open area will contain information that is known by the individual and others; in quadrant two, the blind area, the individual is unaware of information that is known by others; in quadrant three, the hidden, the individual has information that is not shared with others; and quadrant four, the unknown, contains information that is as yet unknown to the individual and others. The premise of this model is that we should be aiming for a situation where quadrant 1 is growing at the detriment of others, because open shared communication is the best way to achieve effective working relationships.

Feedback has a key role here in widening the first quadrant. Feedback from others to an individual, from manager to employee, for example, can reduce the blind area in quadrant 2. The individual can gain greater self-awareness and use this knowledge to improve performance moving forward. We have discussed the importance of two-way feedback. Feedback that is managed as a dialogue rather than purely top-down feedback from manager to individual can enable quadrant 3 to shrink. Others gain a greater knowledge of information held by an individual. For example, a manager may be concerned at an employee's recent, regularly late arrival at work. Rather than chastising the employee a constructive dialogue about the lateness enables the individual to have the confidence to explain a personal issue causing him or her to arrive late. This is more likely to enable a positive action plan to move forward. Again, sharing of information and knowledge should help build trust in the employment relationship.

Praise

One of the most powerful forms of feedback is the simple act of giving people praise. There is a danger that we focus on identifying and dealing with problem areas in employees' performance rather than on ensuring we give positive feedback. Behaviourist theories of learning argue that positive reinforcement is a powerful tool in shaping future behaviours. As Ken Blanchard (2011) has argued: 'catch them doing something right'. It may be that the individual hasn't completely reached the level of performance required, but if we observe them demonstrating behaviours that are moving towards that desired performance we should feed that back to them.

Line managers have a key role in recognizing good performance and achievements in those they manage and delivering positive feedback. The best managers will also ensure that communication of high performance of individuals is fed through to the higher levels of management. One manager I worked with was brilliant at doing this. It only takes a quick phone call or e-mail to make a senior manager aware of an individual's achievement and the same short time for that senior manager to make a call or e-mail the individual to congratulate them. In my personal experience, this kind of feedback is worth its weight in gold in terms of gaining employee commitment and motivation.

Effective feedback

So to summarize, feedback is core to the performance management process. If employees are going to grow in their roles, if they are to deliver the performance required, it is important that they understand on an ongoing basis how they are performing. Employees need to learn in order to be able to grow and improve their performance. Feedback is an important activity in that process, facilitating the opportunity to reflect and learn from day-to-day experiences of carrying out jobs in the workplace. Feedback also is important for motivation, helping to create an environment where employees are more likely to be motivated to perform.

Top tips for giving feedback

Feedback is much more likely to be effective and encourage high levels of performance when it is:

- regular (provided on an ongoing continuous basis);
- timely (particularly with any critical incidents);

- accurate and evidence-based;
- objective (more than one source of feedback);
- constructive;
- invites self-appraisal (how do you think that went?);
- given against a backdrop of trust between parties;
- focused on behaviour not personality;
- achievement is recognized as well as areas for development/ improvement;
- resourced appropriately.

Line managers and the link between feedback and engagement: a viewpoint by Charlotte Martin, HR Consultant

Charlotte Martin, FCIPD, runs her own HR consultancy, Charlotte Martin HR Ltd, and is also an Associate of the CIPD. She guest lectures at Birmingham City University on postgraduate courses on Managing Performance and Reward and has supported clients from a variety of different industries including the NHS, civil service and private companies on refining their approaches to managing performance. Prior to running her own business, she headed up the Reward and Recognition function in the largest Local Authority in Europe.

The role that line managers have to play in performance management is pivotal and, in my experience, the real added value will come from their ability to deliver meaningful feedback. I have held dozens of conversations with industry experts and HR professionals across all sectors and without exception all agree that the skills and abilities of the line manager to have a meaningful dialogue with their team members (including delivering feedback) is key to improving performance. Feedback should be regular and timely as employees need to know when they are doing a great job and the value they are adding to the organization. They also need to know when things aren't on track, and managers need to have the skills and behaviours to handle difficult conversations.

In 2014 the CIPD published some research that highlighted the link between the manager's role and high levels of engagement (CIPD, 2014b). This paper outlined some key research that supported this, including the Engage for Success report (Engage for Success/Rayton et al 2012), which provides some interesting data linking higher employee engagement to improved customer service, lower absence, greater retention as well as higher levels of creativity.

We are really waking up to the significant value of the role line managers play in engagement and performance management, so how can HR help enable and support?

HR has a significant role to play to support organizations and can impact in multiple ways:

- Provide effective and fit for purpose performance management processes.

- Enable the design of infrastructure and systems to support ease of use and recording for managers.

- Review resourcing and talent development strategies to ensure that management and leadership roles include assessment of those soft skills essential for giving feedback, and developing performance with individuals.

- Review learning and development strategies and programme content to assess whether it's fit for purpose.

Over the past few years, I've designed and delivered a number of development programmes to support managing performance for clients across several sectors. What's proved to be really impactful and received high levels of positive feedback has been to really emphasize the impact of the line manager's role in engaging and managing performance with employees. I've done this in two key ways:

1 *To emphasize the cost of employees to the organization* (as in most organizations employees are the highest-costing resource) and highlight the sound business justification to ensuring they are managed and engaged. For example, you wouldn't spend £50,000 on a car and then ignore its maintenance and services or neglect to fill it with oil or check the tyre pressure as you know this would decrease its value and its performance. So why would you recruit someone on a salary of £50K but then not establish expectations and leave them to their own devices (which may not be the same goals as the organization) without checking in on them regularly? It makes sense to look after the most valuable asset.

2 *Emphasizing the link managers have to engagement* and highlighting the impact that disengaged employees bring to the organization. I have found that highlighting some of the negative impacts, particularly the

financial and time-consuming ones, can really make managers and leaders stand back and think. For example, in the State of the Global Workplace Survey (Gallup, 2013) there are some startling statistics on the negative impact of disengaged employees on customer service, productivity and absence. Once you've got their attention you can then make the links to how regular interactions with their team members can make a difference and talk them through the processes and systems available to support them.

Giving feedback can be anything from a simple thank you for a job well done to undertaking more structured discussions. Never forget to recognize good-quality work and behaviours and be prepared to have those difficult conversations; it comes with the job and the skill in delivering constructive feedback to impact on improving performance is extremely valuable and actually very rewarding.

Development, coaching and mentoring

Development

A key aim for performance management is to improve the performance of all employees across the entire organization. An important activity in facilitating this improvement is that of development. An organization should have a clear development policy with effective procedures and activities to support the development needs of employees. The capabilities of teams and individual contributors should be developed in order to achieve the goals of the organization. Performance management should set standards for performance and provide effective mechanisms for review of performance. These activities will particularly identify development needs to support effective performance, so there needs to be a clear flow of communication and data from the performance management process into any development plans and activities.

It is frustrating how many organizations have good performance review processes in place, yet any development needs identified fail to be communicated effectively to those who can take action to meet those needs. This is frustrating for managers, but also demotivating for the individuals concerned. As discussed in Chapter 3, horizontal integration is vital here. If those responsible for learning and development in organizations are working in a silo with poor communication with other areas of the organization, it is likely that performance management will be poorly supported.

Personal development plans (PDPs)

Many performance management processes include the use of personal development plans. These are used to encourage learning and the continuous improvement of performance. They identify development needs and set learning objectives. A plan is worked out to meet those learning objectives, identifying costs, timescales and support required. A variety of development methods may be used, which should be chosen with consideration to the nature of the learning objective, the individual's learning style and the practical issue of resources such as time and money.

It is important that employees 'own' these personal development plans. They shouldn't be imposed by a manager. The manager is there to guide, encourage and support individuals in formulating and implementing the plans. This links to the concept of self-determined learning sometimes referred to as heutagogy. Here you can see the line manager as a 'facilitator' of learning, but the individual takes responsibility for determining their learning plans, choosing the 'what to learn' and the 'how to learn' to meet current and future needs. Self-reflection is an important element of self-determined learning and a key part of PDPs is effective reflective practice. The ability to reflect is important for the learning process – self-reflection and reflection and support from others such as the line manager. Reflection is often the 'missing link' in organization learning today, with mistakes being made or successes being enjoyed without time being made to identify what could be learnt from those experiences and how that learning could be used moving forward. PDPs are a tool that can support this reflection; however, commitment from the organization and the individuals in it to giving time for reflection is the only way to truly close the 'missing link'.

Coaching and mentoring

In recent years there has been a shift away from the narrow concept of providing training in the workplace, to the wider concepts of development and learning. Identifying training needs and courses that will meet those needs usually encompasses only a small part of an individual's development in the workplace. As Kolb's experiential learning model (1985) has taught us, we learn through doing and reflecting: this positions on-the-job learning, facilitated and supported by line managers, as a key development area in the workplace.

Armstrong (2009) identified coaching as a fundamental performance management activity, very much focused on opportunities for learning that emerge through the day-to-day activity of carrying out a job. There are various definitions of coaching, but most identify a one-to-one relationship, often with the line manager, which is focused on encouraging learning and development and an improvement in performance. Coaching is usually seen as a short-term intervention focused on the development of a specific skill or competence. Line managers are very much facilitators of the learning process, not telling individuals what to do, or how to do something, but encouraging them to find their own solutions. Good coaches are excellent listeners and have strong feedback skills. Coaching is an incredibly valuable resource for organizations. Cost-effective, relevant training in being a coach is itself a developmental opportunity for a line manager.

Mentoring is a distinct activity from coaching and is usually undertaken by someone other than an individual's line manager. A typical mentoring relationship is one where a more senior or more experienced member of staff provides support, help and advice to a more junior member of staff. Rather than being focused on short-term skill development, mentoring is often focused on longer-term broader holistic career development for an individual. For example, I was given a mentor who was on the board of the organization I worked for, with a view to help me prepare for promotion on to the board. This had nothing to do with developing HR knowledge or skills needed for my everyday work, but was about developing and exploring areas such as networking, presentation and facilitation skills, and strategic management. It was about equipping me with the confidence and broader business skills to take the next step up. This mentor wasn't my line manager but was an experienced board member who could provide me with support and guidance. In taking the role of mentor, this board member was also being given a developmental opportunity at a time when he had reached a ceiling of development in other areas.

Activity
Personal development planning in practice

Identify an individual that you manage who you believe would benefit from some help with their personal development planning (you may find it beneficial to undertake this activity for yourself if you do not have another employee in mind). Find some time to sit down with the employee and work with them on the activities given below. Ask them to think back over the last six months in their job and identify three occasions when they feel that they really learnt something from the following situations:

- a planned activity – possibly a training course;

- a mistake, or something that did not go well or to plan;

- a success, something that went well.

Ask them to consider the three occasions they have identified and write down what they feel they have learnt from those situations. When you have done that, work with them to set some SMART targets that outline how they could use that learning in their jobs moving forward. It is important that they drive this process, but you have an important role here to support and provide guidance when needed.

Now ask them to consider the next 6 to 12 months in their job. What do they need to be able to do, or need to know to help them improve their performance and develop their career? Help them to identify three areas of learning to support them in achieving that development. How will they achieve that learning? Will it be through experiences on the job, or a formal training intervention, or through the support of a coach or a mentor? Help them with this by outlining what the organization is able to resource. Ask them to write up the learning targets, with ideas of how they will achieve them. Ask them to think about what resources they might need (time, money, support from you/the organization) and then ask them to set a realistic time frame for achievement.

Moving forward you should encourage them to keep a record of their learning on a regular basis (ideally every month). Encourage them to regularly monitor progress against the development plan, removing those areas achieved and adding new targets for learning to support their continuous professional development. Finally, find a mutually agreed time when you will meet to review and discuss progress against the development plan.

In this chapter we explored some of the key activities that form part of the performance management process. The performance agreement provides an important framework within which employee performance is managed. This should be a 'live document' that should be subject to ongoing review and not filed away in an HR database and forgotten!

You should now have a strong sense of the role and impact of effective objective setting, competencies and feedback in the performance management process, and also the importance of strong links with employee development activity to drive continued improvement in employee performance moving forward.

In the next chapter we explore approaches to measuring and evaluating performance, strategies for dealing with the underperformer and the area of absence management.

Measurement

07

In order to be able to manage performance effectively there needs to be clarity in terms of what is expected, and there need to be appropriate measures in place by which we can analyse the degree to which the performance expectation is being achieved. This chapter explores the role of measurement in performance management: the types of measures that may be used, methods of obtaining data for measurement, the use of ratings and their link to reward. In the second part of the chapter we explore how to manage underperformance and manage absence in organizations.

Setting SMART objectives, as discussed in the previous chapter, can certainly improve the objectivity and effectiveness of measurement. As with any type of evaluation, clarity in terms of what should be achieved should provide a strong foundation for any analysis of performance. In some cases, objectives can be set that are fairly easy to measure, based on clear quantifiable data; however, this isn't always so. Some aspects of performance are harder to measure and involve more qualitative data, but these may form a critical part of the analysis of performance. Whilst the process of measurement may have its challenges, relevant, fair measures, closely aligned to the delivery of good performance have an important role in effective performance management.

Decisions need to be made as to what to measure and a good guiding principle here is to measure what is important to the organization and what the organization really values in its employees. By taking the time to measure an aspect of performance the organization is sending out a message that a particular activity or behaviour is important and valued. Some organizations I have come across spend a lot of time measuring things, but there is not always clarity in terms of why or what value is being added by capturing the data. Whatever measures are chosen they need to be meaningful, objective, fair and provide accurate data. It is also important that the measures chosen can be appropriately resourced by the organization:

- Do your line managers have the appropriate capabilities to analyse performance in relation to these measures?

- Is there enough time and money available to justify the use of such measures?

- Is there the appropriate information technology and data capture for the measures identified?

Obtaining data for measurement

Types of measures

Armstrong (2009) suggests that the assessment of performance should be balanced between the following criteria:

- achievements in relation to objectives set;

- the level of knowledge and skills possessed and applied;

- behaviour in the job as it impacts on performance (competencies);

- the degree to which behaviour upholds the core values of the organization;

- day-to-day effectiveness.

This suggests a wide, holistic analysis of performance that takes into consideration both input and output, both behaviours and results. This reflects the concern of recent years with performance management, which is focused too much on short-term results rather than long-term sustainability. In particular, a focus on upholding the core values of the organization and identification with a shared purpose is a theme present in much contemporary research about long-term sustainable business performance. Measures largely fall into two categories: those that focus on an output or outcome (result) and those that focus on behaviours.

Productivity measures

Here, performance is assessed simply in terms of the numerical output of performance. For example, if we were to take the example of someone working in a factory making sandwiches, their performance could be assessed purely on the number of sandwiches made in a set period of time. As long as those sandwiches were basically fit for purpose, the quality of them might be relatively unimportant. In companies where competitive advantage comes through cost, there may well be a primary focus on productivity measures rather than quality. Generally these measures are fairly straightforward to use and assess, with less room for debate around these clearly quantifiable result areas.

Quality measures

For many performance areas it is not sufficient to look purely at numerical output but also the quality of output. An assessment of quality can often be a more subjective process than that of assessing pure numerical output; however, when clear assessment criteria or standards are provided, that subjectivity can be significantly reduced.

Behavioural measures

Competencies have been explored in depth in the previous chapter and we have identified the importance of assessing not just the 'what' of performance, but the 'how'. The focus here is on assessing the behaviour of an employee and looking in detail at how they achieve the output required.

Team measures

In some types of work it is appropriate to focus on team-centric goal-setting. Sometimes an individual's performance is the main force in delivering a good outcome, but in other cases teamwork may be much more significant in delivering high performance. Team-based measures can also be used as a developmental tool to improve collaboration.

Contemporary measures

In recent years performance assessment has started to widen to consider not only an individual's contribution to their specific role, but to the organization in general and even the wider community. It has been argued that to deliver sustainability and competitiveness in performance, a wider perspective needs to be taken and that the true value of an employee to an organization goes beyond their performance of a particular task. The following are some examples of areas of performance where added value might be identified:

- *Organization citizenship behaviour*

  There are many definitions of organization citizenship behaviour (OCB), but for me this is about behaviour contributing to the success and well-being of the organization that goes beyond the basic task requirements of the role. An example of OCB might be supporting others in your team by putting their needs before your own in a particular situation when you know it is for the wider good. It might be putting in extra effort to raise the morale of the team you are working in, maintaining positivity against a backdrop of challenges or disappointments.

- *Contributing to corporate social responsibility initiatives (CSR)*

  Active participation in the organization's CSR initiatives, such as volunteering in the local community, may be an area of performance that an organization wishes to measure. Whilst not directly impacting on the performance of the organization, contributions to such activity may work towards enhancing the employer brand and the wider image of the organization in the community in which it operates. So, measuring an individual's performance in this area, sending out a message that it is valued and important to the organization, may encourage contributions from staff who support and enhance the organization's positive image in the community.

- *Ethical performance*

  Increasingly, both within and outside of the organization, there are strong expectations that employees and organizations will perform ethically. Key performance indictors here would be that the individual operates transparently, honestly and is fair to others in the workplace. This might be a particularly useful area of performance to assess for the leaders/managers in your organization, using 360-degree feedback to capture the assessment information. Again, this could be seen as a fairly subjective area to evaluate; however, clear examples of behaviour will support an objective assessment.

Obtaining data

Whatever measures are used, there needs to be effective processes in place to gather data for those measures so that a meaningful assessment of performance can be made and helpful feedback can be given to the individual. Sources of performance data may include:

- *Business results*

  Obviously the specifics will depend on the nature of your organization, but typical examples might be sales figures, customer feedback, or creative awards. In the area of HR, it might be results in terms of service level agreements (see Chapter 8).

- *Observation*

  A variety of personnel may be involved in the observation of an individual employee's performance, but typically it will be done by the line manager. This approach is particularly helpful when assessing behaviours. It is very important for managers to identify and record specific examples of behaviours in order to provide robust feedback informally on an ongoing basis and formally during the performance appraisal process. Specific examples are more likely to gain employee acceptance of the feedback being delivered.

- *360-degree feedback*

  Again, very helpful in assessing behaviours and for gaining a different perspective on an employee's performance.

- *Critical incidents*

  Here, rather than gathering general data on performance through feedback and/or observation, there is a focus on specific incidents or areas of the job that are considered to be particularly important to successful performance in the job. A good example of a critical area of performance would be 'dealing with a customer complaint'. A focus on critical incidents is often seen to offer value in situations where timescales and resources are tight and a few key areas of the job have a significant impact on overall performance.

- *Data from learning and development interventions*

  Data gathered from learning and development activities can also provide important information in assessing an individual's performance. In general terms it can demonstrate the degree to which an employee is committed to their own continuous professional development. It can also identify the skills, knowledge and behaviours that have been developed by an individual over a given period of time. This data may link to specific learning and development objectives that have been set for the individual and may form part of their continuous professional development plans. It may also provide important data on individuals' readiness for promotion or a different role within the organization. This can then be captured in internal succession planning/talent management activity.

Reflective activity

Think about your own role at work.

- What measures are currently used to assess your performance?
- Can you identify any others that could be helpful moving forward? (Consider different types of measure: productivity, quality, behavioural.)

- If you work in a team are there any team-centric measures you can identify that would be helpful?
- How easy is it to obtain the data to support these measures?
- What resources would you need in your organization to support the use of these measures and how would you justify that investment?

Ratings

There is an ongoing debate about the value of using ratings in the management and assessment of performance in the workplace. Over recent years there has been a shift away from the use of ratings, but for many organizations they are still seen as a critical tool, particularly when there is a strong link to reward decisions but in others, capturing the essence of someone's performance in a single number or letter is felt to be an anathema.

Typical arguments for the use of ratings are as follows:

- Ratings can send a clear message to individual employees about how their performance in the job is viewed and ensure they know when they are considered to be underperforming. Less succinct feedback may leave room for confusion or doubt.
- They provide a helpful way to analyse and categorize performance in the organization. For example, performance ratings may be drawn into an overall employee report, which shows that 20 per cent of the staff are in the 'high-performing' sector and 10 per cent are currently assessed as 'underperforming'. This can also provide useful comparisons between areas of the business and may indicate that certain departments are high-performing and others underperforming.
- In terms of administration it is fairly straightforward to link a number or grade into a financial reward process.
- Ratings can act as motivators, the need for achievement pushing individuals to strive for a higher rating, particularly when there is a clearly understood link to reward or career development opportunities.

Typical arguments against the use of ratings are as follows:

- It isn't possible to capture the essence of someone's performance in a single number or grade. It is an over-simplification, and where the rating refers to average or below average performance this may well have a significant detrimental impact on the morale and motivation of that employee.

- It may lead to some employees leaving a performance assessment focused on a single number, rather than taking on board the more detailed feedback that has been given during the assessment. The focus on a rating linked to reward may also frustrate the developmental aspects of any performance review.

- Managers may have different perspectives on what performance at different rating levels looks like. For example, some managers may very freely give out ratings of outstanding, whereas other managers may very rarely use that level of rating. This can lead to a situation where an employee's performance grade is less dependent on their performance and more on the manager they are reporting to.

- Some rating scales, particularly those comprising an odd number of ratings such as 1–5, allow if not indeed actively encourage, managers to drift towards middle marking. This is sometimes referred to as the 'sitting on the fence' rating: choosing the middle area of satisfactory performance in order to avoid any difficult discussions or action steps related to rating an individual as underperforming.

Ratings are usually assessed and allocated by managers and those managers will have their own biases. As indicated, some managers may have a tendency to generally rate employees kindly, and others may rate employees much more harshly. Some managers dislike and actively avoid conflict of any nature. As indicated above, these managers will seek what they perceive to be the easy route of non-confrontation by avoiding negative ratings and instead giving a central rating. Furnham (1997) identified some typical perceptual errors that may also impact on managers during the rating process, three of which are listed below:

- *Recency effect* – an example of this would be a manager who lets a recent incident or performance issue relating to an employee cloud the entire rating process rather than taking a holistic evaluation of performance over the relevant time period.

- *Contrast error* – rather than looking at an employee's performance objectively against the criteria, the manager may compare them to other members of the team. For example, there may be someone in the team who is consistently exceeding expectations and this may make another employee look as if they are underperforming when actually they are meeting expectations.

- *Halo or horns effect* – a manager allows one negative or one positive aspect of an employee's performance to cloud the overall ratings rather than taking an objective stance across the whole area of performance.

A CIPD Research Report (2016a) recommends employers carefully consider the causes of bias when using ratings. It highlights three types of bias. Firstly, bias in the manager, for example, when the manager hired the employee they may therefore have an invested interest in their success. The second type of bias is due to employee actions, for example, the report highlights political behaviour such as self-promotion potentially leading to higher ratings. Finally, some bias can occur due to the rating system itself, for example, a process that lacks a clear purpose, or managers not being given effective training in the use of rating. Training for managers and ensuring more than one individual feeds into the rating process will improve the objectivity and accuracy of the rating process and outcomes. What is clear is that for ratings to work well, they need to be seen as fair, equitable and based on an objective assessment of performance.

Types of rating scale

Language

There is a good deal of debate around the appropriate language to use for rating scales. Some are defined alphabetically (using a, b, c, for example), others use numbers (1, 2, 3) and others full or abbreviated words either standing alone or linked to a letter or number. Whatever language is used, the hierarchy of ratings is usually fairly easy to identify. There has been a shift away from those scales that are versed from a very positive high rating to a negatively worded lower rating such as 'unacceptable'. Instead many ratings scales today aim to consistently use more positive, encouraging language such as 'basic' or 'developing' to describe performance below satisfactory. I find that managers have mixed feelings about this. Some managers feel that words such as 'unacceptable' send out a much clearer message to employees that they are underperforming and need to improve. Those who prefer the more positive language emphasize that performance management should be about improving performance – and to achieve that improvement in performance, employees need to be encouraged and motivated, not disheartened or demotivated, which may happen when they are rated as 'unacceptable' or 'below average' performers. As with other areas of performance management, the language used is likely to reflect the prevailing culture and management style of the organization.

General performance-rating scale

This is a very simple method whereby the manager is asked to select a rating using a particular scale to indicate the employee's overall performance. This can be highly subjective, particularly where the checking and control methods (as explored below) are not in place. Managers may struggle to find an overall rating, particularly in situations where some areas of an employee's performance are particularly good and other areas quite weak.

Objective-based rating scale

To improve the objectivity of the process, these types of scales require the manager to rate an employee on a scale relating to the degree to which a particular objective has been achieved. Objectivity will be enhanced by effectively worded objectives (SMART), with clearly identified criteria for success in place.

Rating scales that are points-based

Points are allocated to the different parts of the job that the employee carries out. Graded statements indicate how successfully the employee has fulfilled each of the main areas of their job description. This provides a more holistic understanding of the employee's performance and can show where particular strengths in performance lie and also those performance areas that need to be improved or developed.

Behaviourally-anchored rating scales

Behaviourally-anchored rating scales (BARS) provide specific behavioural descriptions to define each of the points on a scale. These are aimed at improving the objectivity of any decisions on ratings. Because behaviours are clearly described, this system is targeted at getting managers to assess specific work behaviours rather than a subjective judgement on personality. Because of the level of detail involved they are time-consuming to develop, but once in place can offer objectivity to the assessment process.

Behavioural observation scales

These are scales developed around statements that summarize desirable or undesirable behaviour. They are often based around critical incidents such as 'deals with customer complaints promptly and effectively'. Usually the assessor will use a Likert scale to assess the statement, where 1 may equate to 'never observed' and 5 'always'. Managers should be recording instances when they have actually observed the employee engaging in the relevant behaviour. This process should encourage managers to record specific examples to support assessment decisions.

General performance-rating scale

TABLE 7.1 Examples of ratings scales

TABLE 7.1A General performance-rating scale

Outstanding	Employee consistently exceeds performance expectations. Employee demonstrates exceptional performance levels or unique contributions to role.
Above standard	Employee demonstrates a high level of performance in many areas.
Satisfactory	Employee's performance is of a satisfactory and acceptable level.
Needs improvement	Employee's performance does not consistently meet expectations. There are some areas of performance requiring improvement/development.
Poor	Employee's performance consistently falls short of that required. Significant areas of performance require improvement/development. A timescaled, resourced plan to address underperformance must be jointly agreed.

TABLE 7.1B Objective-based rating scale

Exceeds	Employee has exceeded the performance level required to meet objectives set.
Met	Employee has fully met the objectives set.
Mostly met	Employee has met most of their objectives, but there are some areas where performance needs to be improved/developed.
Below standard	Employee has failed to achieve a significant number of their objectives and a performance improvement plan needs to be agreed moving forward.

Fairness, equity and effectiveness

All of the above methods of rating performance have advantages and disadvantages. Some may offer ease of implementation but may suffer from an over-simplification and a lack of objectivity. Across all of these methods there are certain activities an organization can put in place that can improve the likelihood of fairness and equity (perceived and otherwise) and the overall effectiveness of the rating of performance.

Training

Training can begin from the point at which line managers are involved in the development of any performance rating system. Input into the design of the system will heighten understanding and hopefully ensure greater commitment to the process. Managers need to be clear what any rating means in terms of actual performance in the job and there should be an agreement of understanding between managers. Training can be given in terms of managing observations and capturing the data/evidence that is required to support objective rating decisions.

Calibration

Many organizations have processes in place for the calibration of ratings. Meetings are held, often facilitated by a senior manager, where managers will come together for the purpose of sharing and reviewing each other's ratings. During these sessions, patterns of ratings will be looked at, for example why does one manager have 70 per cent of employees performing above average to excellent, whilst another only 50 per cent? Does this reflect a clear differential in the performance of their two teams, or is it more a reflection of the manager's style or approach? Where anomalies are found these can be explored and it may be that some ratings will need amending and further training/coaching given to a particular manager. It is important that all staff are aware of this calibration process taking place, as it offers reassurance for all employees regarding fairness and equity.

Monitoring and evaluation

Calibration forms part of the monitoring process, but it is also important for the distribution of ratings to be reviewed on a regular basis by the

HR function. They should look out for anomalies and any unusual patterns from the norm. Gaining employee feedback on the rating system (via surveys or interviews, for example) can also be a helpful tool in assessing the effectiveness and perceived fairness of the process.

Forced ranking

A rather more controversial tool aimed at achieving consistency is that of forced ranking. Managers are required to distribute ratings into a predefined distribution ranking; the aim is to get what is believed to be a 'proper' distribution of ratings and overcome the problem of central marking. Forced ranking aims to gain a true picture of how employees are performing in relation to each other and to drive higher levels of performance across the organization. From a positive perspective it can be used as a tool to highlight top performers, for example, identifying those suitable for inclusion in a management development, or talent management programme. It can also be used to identify the worst performers so that the appropriate action can be taken to address their underperformance (see below). One of the executives most often associated with forced ranking is Jack Welch, retired CEO of General Electric (GE). GE used this tool to move the bottom 10 per cent of performers out of the organization every year! Typically, organizations using forced ranking require their managers to place those they manage in categories and with percentages such as these below:

- top performers should make up only 15 per cent of whole cohort;
- middle performers good/average to make up 70 per cent;
- 15 per cent of performers should be in below average or underperforming.

Whilst forced distribution does achieve a certain level of consistency and highlights high performers and underperformers, the feedback I have received from HR and line managers in organizations who have used this system has been largely negative. Managers have fed back that they felt constrained by having to place people in categories that didn't fully reflect the full spectrum of performance levels and employees found it deeply demotivating. Other negative outcomes highlighted were reduced productivity and collaboration. Whilst the jury is still out in terms of how effective such systems are in driving high performance, CIPD research (2016a) recommends avoiding the use of forced ratings because 'it generates negative employee reactions'. A range of high-profile organizations such as Microsoft and even General Electric have now dropped the use of forced rankings and I would recommend not using them unless you have identified a clear rationale/benefit in doing so.

Ratings and reward

The link between performance management and reward, and the debate regarding the nature of that link, has been discussed earlier in Chapter 3. Ratings can be linked to reward in a variety of ways. They may drive a base pay increase, or be directly linked to some kind of bonus/performance-related payment, for example. The most important thing to ensure with any link between ratings and reward is that it is seen to be procedurally fair. Here are some questions to consider when assessing whether your organization operates fairly on this:

- Is there robust, accurate data driving the rating?
- Is there a consistency of approach across the organization (and particularly between managers)?
- Are rating decisions made objectively?
- Is there the ability for rating decisions to be challenged, reviewed and changed if found to be unsound?

Even when ratings are given that are not what an employee hoped, they are less likely to feel aggrieved than when they feel the actual process has been procedurally unfair. The job of a manager is also made easier when they are working with a rating process that is seen to be procedurally fair; it is more likely that they will gain acceptance of their rating decisions.

Dealing with underperformance

A critical part of performance management is managing the employee who is underperforming. Some managers choose to ignore performance problems, possibly because of the time involved in resolving them, or to avoid the confrontation that may be involved in tackling the underperformance with an employee. I have also come across managers who do an excellent job at passing a problem employee on to another part of the organization, rather than addressing the underperformance themselves! The reality is that performance problems rarely disappear of their own accord, but instead need a systematic approach to address the issue.

Why is it important to deal with underperformance?

So why is it important to take a systematic approach to the underperforming employee, rather than ignoring the issue or moving the individual into another area of the organization?

Meeting organization performance goals

The most obvious reason for dealing with underperformance is the critical link between the performance of the employee and the performance of the organization. If employees are not delivering against their objectives, or are not demonstrating the required behaviours, then the team is unlikely to be performing to the required performance level and ultimately the organization may struggle to achieve its goals. At the heart of performance management is the belief that everyone can and should contribute to the goals of the organization: if that isn't happening at employee level, it will in some way impact on the overall organization performance.

Duty of care

Organizations have a 'duty of care' to their employees. Duty of care means doing all that the organization can to ensure that employees have a safe working environment and that the well-being and health of employees is protected. There is obviously a legal backdrop to this, but there are other business benefits of maintaining a duty of care, linked to productivity, motivation and commitment, reduced absence and staff turnover. There are many aspects to the duty of care, but in terms of performance management key factors in delivering that duty of care are:

- clarity in terms of performance expectations;
- providing regular feedback on performance;
- providing reasonable support to help ensure employees can meet performance requirements.

An underperforming employee needs to know that they are not meeting the required standards of performance. They need to be given clear information to establish in what areas of their performance there is a shortfall. They need to be given the opportunity to discuss and agree methods to overcome the shortfall and be supported in addressing that shortfall moving forward. Uncertainty and a loss of control are significant contributing factors to stress in the workplace; effective performance management can minimize those factors.

Impact on others

An underperforming employee will impact on the various stakeholders in that individual's performance: the manager, other team members, direct reports and indeed customers or clients. Not addressing underperformance is not only unfair on the individual, it is also unfair on those who have a stake or an interest in the employee's performance. Consider the following scenario.

Scenario

Sarah supervises a team of four administrators for a school within a college of further education. The team supports the school well and Sarah is very pleased that her team delivers against their objectives consistently. Sarah is aware that whilst three administrators are high-performing, the fourth, Louise, is often behind with her workload, is rather chatty and sometimes comes in late. Louise is a popular member of the college, always seems to know what is going on and is quite outspoken in her views on college life. Sarah knows she ought to tackle Louise about her underperformance, but she is nervous about tackling such a strong, popular character. Sarah also knows that the other three administrators always pick up any workload that Louise falls behind with. Sarah tends to go to one of the three high performers when she has any additional work that crops up, as she knows they will take it on board willingly.

Time moves on – Sarah avoids the issue and Louise continues to underperform. In the short term all is well, but slowly Sarah becomes aware that the performance of the other three administrators is starting to slide. When she goes to them with any additional work they either say they are too busy, or very grudgingly take it and then take much longer to complete the task than they had previously. Sarah starts to get negative feedback from the rest of the school about the attitude and performance of her team.

The above scenario demonstrates the negative impact on others of not dealing with an underperforming employee. High performers will carry an under-performer for a short period, particularly when there is a reasonable backdrop to that underperformance, such as being a new member of staff, or a temporary health issue. However, it is not a situation that high performers will toler-ate in the longer term, particularly when the underperforming employee is felt to be taking advantage of the high performance and goodwill of others within the team. Two concepts can be usefully applied in relation to this scenario. First, 'social loafing': this refers to the situation where individu-als exert less effort in a group than they would if they were working as an individual. They may exert less effort as they know they will be 'carried' by other members of the team and their lack of effort masked. This in turn leads to the second concept, the 'sucker effect': this is when members of the team, on realizing that they are 'carrying' a team member, choose to reduce their effort and performance. They don't wish to be taken advantage of and therefore reduce their effort accordingly.

The situation in the scenario above can also be related to the equity theories of motivation discussed in Chapter 2. The three team members will start to perceive that despite their performance 'inputs' being much better than that of the fourth member, the 'outputs' that they receive in return for their efforts are the same as the underperforming employee. What incentive do they have to maintain high levels of performance when all that appears to happen is they pick up additional work and only receive the same 'reward' as the employee they are 'carrying'? As a result, their motivation to perform may gradually decline and certainly their willingness to demonstrate the valuable 'discretionary behaviour' will be greatly reduced – as appears to have happened in the above scenario.

Key stages in managing underperformance

There are five typical stages in effectively managing underperformance. The first stage is to identify the performance shortfall and the second is to work out the reasons behind the shortfall. What is causing the underperformance? Once this has been carried out, the next three stages are to identify and agree a plan to address the underperformance, ensure that plan is adequately resourced and, finally, to monitor and review performance moving forward. Let's look at those stages in more detail.

Identifying the performance shortfall

To address underperformance it is very important that there is clarity in terms of the area of performance in which the individual is underperforming. Here are some examples of areas of underperformance:

- against specific objectives;
- overall productivity;
- quality of output;
- attendance (timekeeping or absence);
- behaviours (for example demonstrating contra-indicators in relation to required competencies).

Once the area of underperformance has been clearly identified, accurate data (see above) or specific examples need to be provided to demonstrate why the individual is considered to be underperforming in that area. This is important to help ensure the employee clearly understands how he or she is underperforming and also because he or she is much more likely to accept the feedback with clear supporting evidence of the underperformance.

Identifying the reasons for the shortfall

A good approach to take here is a joint problem-solving one, between manager and employee. It may well be that only the employee can shed any real light on the reason for underperformance, for example in the situation where problems outside of work are impacting on performance at work. Here are some typical reasons for underperformance:

1 The employee doesn't fully understand what is expected.

2 The employee doesn't have the competence (knowledge, skill) to do what is expected.

3 Factors outside of the employee's control are impacting on their ability to deliver what is expected (lack resources or influence, for example).

4 The employee doesn't want to perform, or is not motivated to perform.

Identify a plan to address the shortfall

Once the reason for underperformance is agreed, the employee and manager then need to work out a plan that will enable the shortfall to be reduced moving forward. If we take our four examples above, these are some typical approaches that might be taken:

1 If an employee doesn't fully understand what is expected then there is likely to have been a problem with communication between the manager and employee in terms of the required performance outcomes. A typical response will therefore be for the manager to work through expectations with the employee to ensure clarity of understanding. Getting the employee to articulate expectations back to the manager is a useful tool here to ensure the appropriate understanding is in place. Sometimes role-modelling or coaching by the line manager, or other team members, may help develop an understanding of the required performance standard.

2 If an employee lacks the knowledge, skill or appropriate behaviours to perform to the required standard, then there is likely to be a learning need. The type of learning intervention chosen will depend on the specifics of the situation. It may be appropriate to use a structured off-the-job training intervention, or it may be that coaching from a line manager – where the learning takes place whilst carrying out the role – is a more

appropriate response. Increasingly e-learning interventions are also used to close learning gaps. To move forward effectively, it is helpful here to identify a learning and development objective that can be worked towards and assessed after an agreed period of time.

3 Where factors outside the employee's control are impacting on performance then here the manager needs to work out with the employee what work systems/issues are impeding the employee from delivering the required performance. They may lack particular resources, such as suitable technical equipment, IT packages, etc. It may be that there are problems with the design of the employee's job. For example, the job may be unrealistic in terms of responsibilities covered, or it may be that there is an overlap with other employees that is creating tension and confusion (role overload, ambiguity or conflict). It may be that the manager needs to support the employee more in gaining co-operation from other departments when he or she is dealing with more senior members of staff. The issues here are not always obvious and it may take time and commitment from manager and employer to agree issues and determine an appropriate response.

4 Where the employer doesn't want to perform or lacks the necessary motivation/commitment, here the issue relates to the attitude of the employee. The manager needs to work out why the employee does not want to perform, or isn't motivated or committed to delivering the performance required. It may be that the employee doesn't understand the importance of the task. In this situation the manager needs to communicate why the task needs to be done, so that the employee sees the value in completing the task. It may be that there are issues outside of work that are impacting on the employee's performance. A typical backdrop to this is where the previously good performance of an employee suddenly deteriorates relatively quickly. Managers need to offer support in this situation and make reasonable adjustments to expectations where possible, but should also be aware of the limitations of their role. The company may have an employee assistance programme that can support employees with issues they are facing outside of the workplace.

Motivation has to come from the individual employee, but the line manager can work with the employee to identify what could be done to create an environment where an employee is more likely to be motivated to perform. It may be, of course, that the employee just doesn't want to perform despite the organization taking reasonable steps to provide an appropriate working environment. Having been counselled on the consequences of underperformance it may then be appropriate for the organization to shift into a disciplinary procedure to deal with a conduct issue.

Resource strategies to improve performance

When agreeing an action plan to improve performance it is vital that appropriate resources to support the plan are identified and put in place. Without adequate resourcing the plans are likely to fail to turn around performance and employees are likely to lack motivation to perform, as they see the performance targets as unattainable. If we take the four examples above, these are some of the typical resourcing requirements:

1 *The employee doesn't fully understand what is expected* – as the issue here is largely about communication, the main resourcing issue will be the manager's time. In some situations it may be that the manager has not fully understood the required performance outcomes: in this instance a more senior manager's time will be required to ensure clarity of understanding.

2 *The employee doesn't have the competence (knowledge, skill) to do what is expected* – in this second area, the resourcing issues are going to be linked to the learning and development intervention that is chosen to close the learning gap. With coaching it may be the manager's time again, but it might be the cost of a training intervention and the associated time costs of taking the employee out of their day-to-day work, and possibly hiring temporary cover for them while the employee attends any training.

3 *Factors outside of the employee's control are impacting on their ability to deliver what is expected* – in this third area, it may be a question of resourcing the right equipment for the employee to carry out tasks to the required level. If the job needs to be redesigned, this will involve the costs associated with the manager's time, as will additional support for the individual to gain co-operation from other areas of the organization.

4 *The employee doesn't want to perform, or is not motivated to perform* – in this fourth area, we once again have costs associated with the manager's time. There also may be costs linked to counselling support for the employee, or additional resources in terms of the time of other employees to support the employee in their role whilst they are unable to deliver 100 per cent of the job requirements.

Monitor and review

Where there is underperformance it is very important that a process is put in place to monitor and review performance moving forward. The manager should agree timescales for improvement with the employee and these will act as milestones when a review of performance will take place. An underperforming employee shouldn't be left working without feedback until the next formal appraisal, but should receive regular feedback to understand whether they are moving in the right direction to improve performance. It is very important to regularly reinforce behaviours that are moving the individual towards achieving the required performance and to capture behaviours that are not.

Activity

- Identify someone in your organization who you believe is underperforming.

- What area is their underperformance in and what evidence (data, examples) do you have to support the assessment of underperformance?

- What might be the reasons behind the underperformance?

- What plans/strategies might address this underperformance?

- What resourcing will be required to support any intervention to improve performance?

Managing absence

Absence management is a particularly complex area of performance management and as such deserves a separate section here. Absence costs the UK economy many millions of pounds annually and there is strong evidence to show that the best-performing organizations generally have lower absenteeism rates than other organizations. Absence creates significant costs for organizations, not only in terms of loss of productivity, but also the costs of temporary cover and the time needed from managers to manage the absence. The CIPD Absence Management Survey (2016c) reported that over a quarter of respondents stated that absence management was currently amongst their top three greatest people management priorities. Whilst the survey noted a decrease in absence levels to an average level of 6.3 days per employee, the decrease varies across sectors and with the smallest decrease in the public sector. Absence remains costly with median cost of absence per employee of £522 (public sector £835 per employee). There are a range of strategies organizations can employ to manage absence effectively. Some, such as return to work interviews, remain a popular method and have been used in absence management for many years. Others, such as well-being strategies and initiatives, have grown in popularity in recent times.

Policy

As a starting point an organization should have a clear and effectively communicated policy. The policy needs to support the organization's objectives and culture, but also explain the rights and obligations of employees and meet any legal requirements, such as a statement of the arrangements for sick pay. As with other organization policies, an absence policy provides a framework within which the employment relationship is carried out and ensures rights and obligations are clear from the start, which makes the ongoing management of absence a more straightforward task. It is particularly important that managers fully understand the policies and required procedures and have the capability to carry out absence management in a consistent way across the organization. Line managers need ownership of issues relating to absence, with the support of HR. The CIPD (2017d) states that absence policies should:

- provide details of contractual sick pay terms and its relationship with statutory sick pay;
- explain when and whom employees should notify when they are not able to attend work;
- include when (after how many days) employees need a self-certification form;
- contain details of when employees require a 'fit note' from their doctor;
- explain that adjustments may be appropriate to assist the employee in returning to work as soon as is practicable;
- mention that the organization reserves the right to require employees to attend an examination by a company doctor and (with the worker's consent) to request a report from the employee's doctor;
- include provisions for return-to-work interviews;

- give guidance on absence during major or adverse events (for example, snow, pandemics or popular sporting events such as the Olympic Games or World Cup).

Measurement and monitoring

Measuring and monitoring absence rates and the reasons causing absence is a fundamental part of absence management and important for the performance management process. Most organizations should have mechanisms in place to track absenteeism on a weekly or monthly basis. Measurement will often take the form of calculating absence using a formula and comparing the results with internal or external benchmarks. For example, the absence rate is usually calculated as follows:

$$\frac{\text{Number of hours or days absence}}{\text{Number of working hours or days available}} \times 100$$

This can be done on an individual, team or organization-wide basis and shows the percentage of total time available that has been lost due to absence. A limitation of this approach is that it does not show any patterns of absence, for example individuals taking long-term absence or individuals having frequent short spells of absence. Frequency rate calculations provide this, for example:

$$\frac{\text{Number of spells of absence over a given period}}{\text{Number of employees over a period}} \times 100$$

The Bradford Index (below) measures spells of absence and is useful in identifying persistent short-term absences for individuals:

$$S \times S \times D$$

(where S = number of spells of absence in 52 weeks taken by an individual, and D = number of days of absence in 52 weeks taken by an individual)

So, five two-day absences would be $5 \times 5 \times 10 = 250$.
And two five-day absences would be $2 \times 2 \times 10 = 40$.

This index allows organizations to produce a weighted comparative index and HR/management can decide a value, which when hit will action a review of that individual's attendance, such as a formal interview on the subject of their absence level.

The implication here is that the more frequent shorter-term absences have the potential to be more problematic and cause greater disruption for organizations. This fact was highlighted by the Advisory, Conciliation and Arbitration Service (ACAS) in 2013:

> Statistics suggest that long-term absences are more costly to employers than short-term. But short-term absences are arguably more disruptive, particularly for smaller businesses. While cover can often be planned and provisions made during long absences, the sudden upheavals caused by a day or two off here and there can put a strain on colleagues who may have to fill the gaps at the last moment. When it gets more serious, it could affect morale and hit productivity.
>
> (ACAS, 2013)

The Bradford Index and other forms of data capture relating to absence should provide triggers to draw attention to individual, team or organization issues relating to absence. The monitoring and measurement of absence, therefore, forms a vital aspect of effective management.

Identifying the reasons for absence

As well as measuring the amount and frequency of absence, it is also important to capture and monitor the reasons behind absence. This data can be helpful on an individual, team or organization-wide level. For example, a significant amount of absence in a specific department linked to the category of workplace issues (see below) may indicate the need for some action by the organization. It may be that a particular manager has a problematic management style that needs to be addressed in some way. Data providing detail on the reasons for absence can be captured in a variety of ways:

- *Absence notification procedures*
  Organizations should have clear procedures in place for employees to report their absence to the organization. When the absence is reported it is also important that the reason for absence is identified and, if possible, an idea of the timing of a return to work. This discussion is important for the effective management of the absence, and organizations report that it is also helpful in minimizing the length of any absence.

- *Ongoing contact during the absence period*
  It is acceptable and advisable to maintain contact with employees during the absence period, to be aware of any changes relating to the absence and maintain a feel for when the employee is likely to be back in the workplace.

- *Return-to-work interviews and formal absence review meetings*
  Return-to-work interviews send out a clear message that absence is taken seriously by the organization. They enable line managers to explore the underlying issues that may be causing the employee to take time out of the workplace. They can help deal with short-term absence issues sooner rather than later.

As with other areas of underperformance, there are a variety of reasons that may lie behind absence and it is important to identify the reason and then work on a suitable response. Reasons for absence can be loosely categorized into four areas:

- Health and general lifestyle factors such as smoking or excessive alcohol consumption, fitness/weight issues and genuine illness.

- Factors relating to the workplace such as workplace relationships, management style, excessive workload, health and safety concerns and bullying.

- Attitudinal issues such as low motivation or a lack of commitment to the job and/or organization.

- Factors in an individual's personal life, such as going through a difficult event such as divorce or bereavement or having challenging care responsibilities such as for an elderly or sick relation or children under 16.

These reasons can lead to a variety of types of absence: short-term absence, long-term absence, unauthorized absence or persistent timekeeping issues such as lateness. There are also various types of authorized absence: for example, annual leave, maternity and paternity leave or compassionate leave – but absence that is given approval in advance is generally less disruptive than absence that is unplanned. In terms of unplanned absence, the type of absence and the reason behind it will require different approaches.

Approaches to managing absence

As well as the mechanisms identified above there are various strategies that organizations can follow to manage absence. Taylor (2008) identifies three approaches: punitive, incentivizing and preventative.

The punitive approach is the most common and uses the measurement processes and management tools such as return-to-work interviews that we have just explored. Whilst the backdrop to all the approaches is definitely welfare, the punitive approach also makes it clear to the employee that their absence has been noted, that absence without good reason is unacceptable and that there is the potential for disciplinary action for persistent absenteeism. There is clearly a complex legal backdrop to this, such as the impact of the Disability Discrimination Act of 1995, which goes beyond the remit of this book. However, it is important to point out here that any action taken needs to make a clear distinction between capability and conduct and needs to be seen as fair and reasonable within the legal backdrop.

Some punitive measures will involve reducing pay, others may relate to decisions about an individual's future employment, such as selection criteria for redundancy or decisions relating to promotion. Despite criticisms of the punitive approach and questions over the effectiveness of such methods, it appears it is still the most commonly adopted way of responding to absence. Such methods are certainly more likely to lead to positive outcomes when they are applied fairly and consistently across the organization.

A rather more controversial approach is where organizations reward employees for good attendance. This might be through attendance bonuses, or an enhancement of a profit-related pay scheme, or some kind of group-based attendance bonus that adds peer pressure as an incentive to attend. Some managers will baulk at the concept of paying people to do what they should be doing anyway, but many organizations report that rewards – both financial and non-financial – in return for good attendance does impact positively on absence levels.

The third approach is that of preventative measures that aim to reduce the root causes of absence in the organization. If we look back at the four typical categories of absence identified above, the following are just some of the many actions and initiatives organizations can take to help reduce absence levels:

- Select people to work for the organization who demonstrate positive work ethics, motivation and commitment, and then aim to create an environment where they are more likely to be motivated to perform.

- Provide training for line managers in good people-management techniques.

- Ensure effective job design that considers the needs of the individual as well as those of the organization.

- Provide occupational health services, counselling sessions or employee assistance programmes.

- Offer flexible working practices.

- Provide healthy living advice/gym membership.

Some of these activities and initiatives bring greater cost implications than others, but good preventative measures can have a very positive impact on attendance levels and therefore are likely to be saving significant costs in terms of future absenteeism. In recent years many of these preventative measures have started to be 'wrapped up' within an overarching Well-being Strategy. The CIPD Survey (2016c) found that nearly half of respondents reported a growth in their organization's focus on well-being. More and more organizations are recognizing that well-being programmes are much more than about preventing absence. They have identified that well-being programmes shaped around the nature of their organization can be a key driver in employee engagement and productivity.

DIAGNOSTIC QUESTIONNAIRE

The following questionnaire (Table 7.2) requires you to evaluate how effectively absence is managed in your organization and to explore typical reasons for absence. To conduct this evaluation fully you will find it helpful to access the following:

- your organization's absence policy;
- any absence reports that have been produced;
- return-to-work interviews;
- sick notes;
- you may find it helpful to talk to line managers and employees about their experiences of absence management.

Particularly where you score your organization's performance as poor or fair, try to identify specific action points to improve future performance.

TABLE 7.2   Evaluating absence management in your organization

1. To what degree does your organization's absence policy meet good practice?   1 = Poor   2 = Fair, areas for improvement   3 = Good   4 = Excellent (What can the organization do to improve?)

(continued)

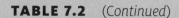

TABLE 7.2 *(Continued)*

2. How well is the organization's absence policy communicated to and understood by the organization? 1 = Poor   2 = Fair, areas for improvement   3 = Good 4 = Excellent (What can the organization do to improve?)
3. How does your organization measure and record absence?
4. How effective are the methods in Q3 in managing absence? 1 = Poor   2 = Fair, areas for improvement   3 = Good 4 = Excellent (What can the organization do to improve?)
5. How does the organization find out the reasons behind an employee absence?
6. How effective are the methods you identified in Q5? 1 = Poor   2 = Fair, areas for improvement   3 = Good 4 = Excellent (What can the organization do to improve?)
7. What do you think are the main underlying causes of absence in your organization?
8. What might be the best approaches or strategies to improve absence levels in your organization?

Presenteeism

It is also worth mentioning that for some organizations, the issue is less about absenteeism, but presenteeism. For many organizations the long-hours culture persists, often led by senior management role-modelling long working days. Presenteeism in recent years is not necessarily about being at your desk, but about having a constant virtual presence for the organization you work for. Responding to e-mails late at night, or at weekends, or while on holiday. The impact of a belief that an employee is 'on-call 24/7' can be a detrimental one to home life and the well-being and possible health of the individual. This might manifest itself in lower performance levels, or eventually may lead to absence from work. The danger of a long-hours culture has been highlighted in recent times with the inquest into the death of a student who collapsed after allegedly working non-stop for 72 hours, nearing the end of a seven-week internship at a London City Bank. Managers should ensure that they take steps to discourage presenteeism – and a good starting point is ensuring that where possible they themselves adopt a positive approach to work–life balance. However, the wider issue here really is the culture of the organization and how behaviours are role-modelled from the top of the organization. Presenteeism is like the flu, it spreads rapidly and works against employee well-being and long-term sustainable performance.

In this chapter we have explored the role of measurement in the performance management process. It is very important for organizations to have a clear understanding of the nature of performance that will drive success. With that understanding in place, data must be captured so that measurement of how the organization is doing can be assessed and strategies developed to ensure a sustainable continuous improvement in performance over the long term.

Monitoring and evaluating the performance of the organization, teams and individuals forms a key part of the performance management process. It is also important that the performance management process itself is monitored and evaluated. This is explored in depth in the next chapter.

08

Conclusion

This final chapter considers how we monitor and evaluate performance management. We will also explore the value of reporting on data captured, both within the organization and externally. In recent years it has become more important than ever to demonstrate the value of an HR intervention, both internally and externally. Back in 1998 David Ulrich described HR as 'value-sapping' and laid down a challenge for HR professionals to demonstrate added value in the workplace, providing a vision of how that might happen in practice. In recent years there has been a clear drive from academics and practitioners alike to push for greater evidence-based HR practice, maximizing the opportunity for value-add impact and strengthening HR's credibility within organizations. The added-value of HR practices such as performance management needs to be clearly identified and communicated to employees, managers, senior management and those beyond the organizations, such as shareholders, clients and customers in whatever sector the organization operates in. Identifying valuable outputs from performance management helps to drive the ongoing involvement in and commitment of the stakeholders in the process. The activities of monitoring and evaluation of performance management are vital in order to be able to demonstrate added value, and they should be treated as ongoing processes in the organization:

> Performance Management processes have to be nurtured. The fundamental mistake many organizations have made is to believe that all they have to do is design an elegant system complete with documentation, to a flourish of trumpets introduce the systems with the help of a glossy brochure, run one or two half-day training courses, and it will all happen as planned... the systematic monitoring and evaluation of performance management... is essential to generate the information required to maintain it as an effective process.
>
> (Armstrong and Baron, 2005)

Monitoring and evaluating performance: why?

Evaluating any HR intervention is not always an easy or straightforward task. HR isn't an 'owned resource' as other resources in the organization and many aspects involve qualitative rather than quantitative data. There are many variables that can impact on performance and it can be challenging to prove definitively that X has caused Y. However, even though the task of monitoring and evaluation and, most importantly, demonstrating a valuable impact may be challenging, it is worth the effort as it can bring many benefits. I found it reassuring that in the CIPD Performance Management Survey of 2009, only 1 per cent of respondents identified performance management evaluation to be too difficult to attempt! I have outlined below some of the benefits of evaluation that I have experienced, or that others have outlined to me from their organization's practices:

- Performance management is more likely to gain the ongoing commitment of senior management to the process where a clear value and contribution to the organization is identified.

- Stakeholders will be happier with any investment into performance management (particularly in terms of their time), when they can see a tangible outcome.

- Future investment in performance management activity is more likely to be forthcoming where added value can be demonstrated.

- Monitoring and evaluation can identify problems enabling suitable action to take place and impeding the progress of small issues into large-scale problems.

- Monitoring and evaluation can identify 'centres of excellence', where good practice can be captured. Good practice can then be shared across the organization, and knowledge and skills in relation to performance management can be strengthened.

- Monitoring and evaluation can help in ensuring that processes and outcomes of performance management are fair, which in turn will help ensure that the company isn't exposed in terms of employment legislation. Fair processes will also help ensure a strong employer brand both within and without the organizations (as discussed in Chapter 2).

Monitoring and evaluating performance: what?

Efficiency, effectiveness and fairness

Whether an organization is evaluating performance management or any other areas of HR activity, it is important that the evaluation doesn't just look at whether goals have been reached. This fails to reflect the wider picture of how those results were achieved. I find it helpful to approach evaluation through three different lenses: evaluating in terms of efficiency, effectiveness and fairness. Let us consider these three areas in more detail:

- Efficiency – this type of evaluation looks at the process, the way an activity (in this case performance management) is carried out. It is important to consider the use of resources here. For example, considering the time taken to complete a process. Also, value-for-money considerations play an important part in this type of evaluation. Do the benefits gained justify the investment made? Objectives may have been achieved, but were the costs involved justifiable? Could the same results have been achieved without the same level of investment in resources?

- Effectiveness – this type of evaluation is concerned with outcomes. Has the process/activity delivered the desired results? To what degree have goals been met? Has the process had the desired impact on organization performance?

- Fairness – this area of evaluation also looks at how the process/activity of performance management has been carried out and the outcomes of the process, but specifically in terms of fairness. Has performance management in this organization been carried out with 'procedural fairness'? Are the outcomes of performance management fair to the stakeholders in the process? Is there 'distributive justice' in evidence?

To bring these three areas to life a little more, consider the following three scenarios.

Scenario

Scenario 1

ABC Engineering has introduced a new 360-degree feedback element into their performance management process. The 360-degree feedback process is working well and useful data is being captured that has helped improve employee performance in many areas. Employees and managers have given positive feedback on the process and it is seen as being a fair process by stakeholders. However, the external consultants employed to introduce 360-degree feedback into the organization were very expensive. There were problems in getting the consultants to fully understand the nature of the business and also problems with the early pilots of the scheme, which meant that full implementation was delayed by about six months.

Scenario 2

ABC Engineering has introduced a new 360-degree feedback process. The design, development and implementation process has been delivered well within set time frames and budgets. The feedback gained from the 360-degree feedback is not of a high quality. People seem either reluctant to offer honest feedback or have been confused by the complexity of language relating to competencies used in the feedback forms. As a result, the data gathered has not been helpful in developing or improving the performance of employees.

Scenario 3

ABC Engineering has introduced a new 360-degree feedback process. Once again the design, development and implementation process has been delivered well within set time frames and budgets. Employees understand the tool and useful data has been captured to develop or improve performance. There is, however, much inconsistency in terms of how individual managers use the data captured to feed into overall performance grades. Some managers give high grades very easily, others are much tougher on their employees. The lack of consistency has caused several grievances to be raised by employees. One employee felt that the feedback given by their manager amounted to a personal attack rather than focusing on working behaviours, and has resigned and is bringing a constructive dismissal case against the organization.

The scenarios outlined above are fairly simplistic in nature, but they highlight why it is important to evaluate in terms of all three criteria of efficiency, effectiveness and fairness. In Scenario 1 the evaluation is likely to show fairness and effectiveness, but may highlight that there were some weaknesses in terms of efficiency, including appropriate selection and use of resources.

In Scenario 2 the evaluation is likely to show efficiency and fairness, but may show that the outcomes are not what was originally hoped for. If we are not doing the right things in the first place we are unlikely to achieve the desired results, however fair or efficient we are being.

In Scenario 3 we can see that efficient and effective is not sufficient. If a process/activity is not perceived as fair this will also be problematic for the organization. Perceived unfairness creates conflict that can be both damaging and time-consuming for the organization and can also impact on the motivation, commitment and overall performance of employees. It can also impact negatively on the employer brand.

Consider what the organization might have done in each of these three scenarios to ensure that the 360-degree feedback process achieved a positive evaluation against all three of the criteria.

Activity

- Identify a process or project you have recently been involved with at work. Now evaluate this project in terms of the three criteria:
  - Efficiency: to what degree was the process/project managed efficiently with appropriate use of resources?
  - Effectiveness: to what extent were the goals or desired outcomes achieved?
  - Fairness: was the process managed fairly and were the end results fair?
- Did the process or project meet all three criteria well, or were some criteria met better than others?
- If there is an imbalance, why do you think this is? For example, was there too great a focus on the end result without enough consideration of the methods used to achieve the result?
- What could be done to improve the evaluation results across the three criteria moving forward?

Areas of evaluation

The nature of your performance management process, its complexity for example, will impact on how you monitor and evaluate and what areas you will choose to evaluate. You may wish to take a holistic approach to evaluation or, where a new element or change has been introduced, for example 360-degree feedback, you may wish to focus evaluation on that one particular element. Evaluation takes time and resources and, because of this, organizations need to be sure that the evaluation will add value. Whilst the nature of evaluation will vary according to the organizational situation, there are however some typical areas that organizations will look at when evaluating their performance management activity. Here are some typical criteria for you to consider:

- Performance appraisals are completed regularly according to the agreed policy. With some organizations moving away from a focus on an annual appraisal, the challenge here will be evaluating the frequency and effectiveness of more regular performance check-ins.

- All employees are working to a set of clearly understood and agreed objectives.

- Employees understand how their role contributes to organization success.

- All employees receive regular feedback on their performance.

- There are effective links between performance management and other HRM areas such as reward, and learning and development, so that an integrated approach is achieved.

- Performance management is carried out fairly and consistently across the organization.

- Performance management supports and drives effective individual, team and organization performance in line with the overall goals of the organization.

This list is not intended as an exhaustive list of areas but as a starting point. How many of these areas do you think your organization currently evaluates performance management against? Where are the gaps? What could the organization do to improve how it evaluates performance management?

Monitoring and evaluating performance: how?

Methods of evaluation

There are a wide range of evaluation tools/techniques available. Once the organization has decided what is important to evaluate, then it can work out which evaluation tool will best support the capture and analysis of data required.

Goal-based

A fairly straightforward method of evaluation is based on setting specific goals for objectives for the performance management process. As with other objective-setting processes, the evaluation is based on an assessment of whether those objectives have been met and how well they have been met. The effectiveness of the evaluation process will be dependent on the degree to which the objectives set have clear criteria for success outlined. The process of evaluation should offer minimal room for subjectivity when clearly defined goals are in place. Examples of performance management objectives could be:

- to ensure no more than 15 per cent of performance reviews are overdue by the end of the month;

- to ensure all completed performance reviews have included a learning and development objective;

- to ensure all new managers have received training in handling performance reviews prior to conducting any reviews of their team.

Benchmarking

Benchmarking involves comparing data on performance management internally (between departments or sites, for example) or with other organizations, either in the same sector or outside it. Internal benchmarking is generally more straightforward, mainly because of access to relevant data. Companies can be reticent to share what may be perceived as competitive data, but others will see an exchange of data as mutually beneficial. Professional bodies such as the CIPD, or the CBI (Confederation of British Industry) are also good sources of data for benchmarking purposes, and there are also private companies that offer benchmarking tools. Some of the consultancies providing benchmarking data have the advantage of holding large databases of organization practices but there are often significant costs in using such data.

However challenging or costly, external benchmarking is worth exploring as a tool for evaluation, as it can provide valuable comparators, particularly when benchmarking against an organization regarded as 'excellent' in a particular area of people management. At the time I worked in the advertising industry, the Institute of Practitioners in Advertising encouraged information sharing on HRM practices between agencies and aimed to provide helpful data for benchmarking purposes. Are there any organizations that could provide benchmarking data appropriate for your organization?

Audit

An audit also involves the process of conducting a comparative analysis. Here, however, rather than making a comparison against a specific organization or organizations, the comparison is made with standards that are considered to be exemplars of good or excellence in practice. If the organization considers itself to be a leader in terms of people management activity, arguably it is less useful to use other organizations as comparators, but better to use exemplars of excellence to enable the organization to continuously improve. This links to the excellence-orientated approach to performance management discussed in Chapter 1. Audit-based evaluation, linked to good practice, also has use in terms of demonstrating fairness and compliance with employment law legislation.

Surveys

Surveys are another useful way of evaluating performance management. Surveys can be targeted at specific areas or conducted as a company-wide survey. They are usually targeted internally within organizations at those who manage or employees. However, customer or client surveys can also provide helpful data to link into the evaluation of the performance management processes. This data may provide helpful evaluation linked to the outputs of performance management in terms of behaviours and results.

Surveys provide a good 'health check' on how performance management is being carried out in organizations – and the output. However, they are sometimes based more on opinions and perceptions rather than hard data and this needs to be taken into account in any evaluation process.

In my experience the most useful surveys are those that are repeatedly conducted over a period of time, annually for example. A single survey provides a snapshot of feedback at one point, but I have found that the really useful data gathered from surveys are those which relate to trends over time. It is particularly helpful to conduct a survey before and after a period of change. For example, in the context of performance management you could conduct an employee survey before and after the introduction of a new performance management process. You can explore how attitudes towards performance management and behaviours have changed over that time. Identifying a positive change in employees' or managers' attitudes towards performance management after a new process has been introduced provides good evidence of commitment and added value, and this can then be evaluated further by looking at whether behavioural change had followed attitudinal change.

Below are some examples of the type of questions you could include in an employee survey and some questions you could use for a survey of the managers in your organization. A Likert scale of measurement, for example 1 = strongly agree, 2 = mostly agree, 3 = partly agree, 4 = partly disagree and 5 = strongly disagree would be appropriate to use against each question.

Example questions for employee survey:

- I am working to an agreed set of objectives.
- My manager gives me regular feedback on how I am performing in my job.
- The feedback I receive is based on fact, not opinion.
- I feel that my achievements are recognized.
- I feel that the outcomes of my annual review are fair.

Example questions for manager survey:

- I have been given adequate training and support to carry out performance management.
- I feel confident in giving feedback to my reports.
- I actively encourage upward feedback during the performance review process.
- I am confident in setting agreed SMART objectives.
- Learning and development needs identified during the performance review process are supported and usually actioned by the organization.
- I believe performance management will enable me to do my job better.

Interviews or focus groups

As discussed in the case study below, interviews ideally structured or semi-structured are useful in gaining feedback on employee and manager experiences of the performance management process. With an interview rather than a questionnaire, there is the opportunity for discussion, probing and clarification of feedback in order to gain a greater depth of understanding.

Focus groups are a type of group interview that will enable the organization to gain information and feedback relating to performance management through group dialogue and discussion. Focus groups enable a range of attitudes and opinions to be explored and are a useful mechanism for capturing qualitative data and drawing out themes. With focus groups and interviews it is important that the interviewer/facilitator is trained to enable appropriate data to be gathered and to ensure participants have a positive experience.

CASE STUDY

Several years ago I was involved in taking an organization through the Investors in People (IIP) accreditation process. The first stage was to evaluate our current practices in performance management. As part of that evaluation we conducted an audit of current practice to assess the organization in how far away it was from achieving the requirements of the IIP standards for accreditation. Activities undertaken as part of that audit process included the following:

- Interviews with a range of staff to ascertain whether they understood how their role linked to the overall goals of the organization.
- Interviews with some of the senior management team to assess their view on and involvement with performance management.
- Use of HR reports to identify status on appraisal completion.
- A review of a sample of completed appraisals to evaluate the quality of completion. For example, evidence of SMART objective setting, and relevant learning and development needs identified.
- A review of learning and development needs identified in appraisal with learning and development activity, to assess whether those needs had been actioned appropriately.

Data gathered during the audit enabled the organization to then identify gaps or shortfalls in meeting the requirements of the IIP standard. The next stage was to then identify appropriate strategies to close those gaps in order to enable successful accreditation, but most importantly to improve the organization's approach to managing performance.

We were also provided with a consultant who worked for an organization that had recently successfully achieved IIP accreditation. She provided a range of benchmarking data so that we could compare our organization practices against those of the organization the consultant worked for. This was particularly helpful in providing my organization with real-life examples of how the IIP standard could be applied in practice. This also helped with challenging any cynicism regarding the practicality of some of the demands of the IIP standards. Being able to provide some real-life examples of organization practices and, most importantly, of the valuable outcomes of those practices, was extremely helpful in achieving senior management support for going through the accreditation process.

The balanced scorecard

In the CIPD Performance Management Survey (2009) most respondents thought that 'effective evaluation can only really occur when there is a clear line of sight between individual effort and contribution and business objectives'. Balanced scorecards, which start at the corporate level then cascade down to functional levels and then into agreed SMART individual objectives have been one way that organizations have approached this.

Originally developed by Kaplan and Norton (1996), the balanced scorecard aimed at widening the focus of companies away from short-term financial reporting to broader measures of performance. Where performance management aligns with the scorecard, we should hope to see an impact not only in terms of financial results, but also on areas such as customer satisfaction, the quality of our internal process and the quality of the human capital in the organization. There is an emphasis on the importance both of quantitative and qualitative data here, in building a true picture of an organization's performance.

Human capital reporting

The collective capability of the people an organization employs, their skills and knowledge is now often referred to as human capital. Introducing measures of human capital can help deliver effective HR/L&D practices and help drive organization performance on a sustainable basis. Here now is a viewpoint on human capital from one of the leading researchers in this area.

Human capital reporting: a viewpoint by Edward Houghton, Senior Research Adviser CIPD

Business leaders commonly refer to the workforce as 'their most important asset' but as CIPD research has shown, annual reports and accounts offer very little insight into what this means in practice. Whilst other asset classes (such as buildings and machinery) are easily valued, depreciated and reported, the more intangible aspects of business such as brand and workforce are omitted from the balance sheet, with broad estimates of value only sometimes being disclosed. And whilst some measures are now being mandated through UK regulation (such as measures relating to the gender pay gap), there are relatively few measures which can commonly be found in FTSE 100 annual reports and account. There are a number of key reasons for this; most prevalent is a lack of consistent measures, which is compounded by unclear or undefined accounting rules, and a bias in annual reports towards measures of short-term value creation and capture. Human capital reporting has for some time been a very small part of reporting practice, but with both understanding of workforce data growing, and interest from stakeholders developing, this is likely to change.

A chequered past

Various national government and professional body initiatives have tried to change this. In 2003 the Accounting for People Taskforce was launched and their later published report attempted to drive organizations towards better reporting. However, by drawing on case studies from the financial services the initiative came under scrutiny following the dissection of banking culture after the 2008 global financial crisis. A similar story of failure by the US Society for Human Resource Management (SHRM) in 2010, which failed to consult adequately with leading HR professionals, meant that again human capital reporting was questioned and sidelined for political reasons.

Building a common language

Since 2013 the CIPD has been investigating human capital reporting theory and practice, describing standard measures for practice and helping to illustrate the value to be gained from reporting workforce concepts such as performance to external stakeholders. The Valuing Your Talent framework, developed with the Chartered Institute of Management Accountants, Chartered Management Institute and Lancaster University Management School, illustrates a set of measures which, if reported, are believed to describe the key concepts external stakeholders should be understanding about the workforce (CIPD, 2014a). The measures to be reported from the framework are contextual and specific to organizations, so no set standard exists, but a number of measures can be used if deemed strategically insightful by an organization. These can include:

- *Input measures*: Inputs are the fundamental building blocks for achieving value through people. This is the most basic level of measures available to an organization. These measures include workforce cost, diversity and inclusion statistics and demographic statistics.

- *Activity measures*: Activities are the key investments and processes that organizations choose to make to ensure their people are able to work productively and healthily. These include measures relating to human resource management systems and processes, including employee reward and workforce planning insights.

- *Output measures*: Outputs are the results of the investments in activity-level processes and provide the means for evaluating the effectiveness of the impact of activities of human resources management. Outputs include workforce performance, productivity and leadership capability.

- *Outcome measures*: The final level of impact from human resource management practices describes the value that stakeholders gain from human resources and workforce practice. This includes value generated through culture, innovation and agility. These measures help to illustrate the strategic impact of human resources practice.

Measures from all of these areas of HR enable external stakeholders to understand how the workforce is being managed and developed to deliver value to the organization's stakeholders, which should include employees. Further research by the CIPD in 2016 found that there are clear areas of improvement needed within the human capital reporting space, in particular the extent to which measures are transparent and accurate, for example some organizations were shown to be misreporting or under-reporting workforce risks to their stakeholders, a potential issue that could seriously damage trust in business (CIPD, 2016b).

Performance management: a question of measurement and narrative

Performance management and its outcomes are clear measures of interest to external stakeholders because they offer insights into both the quality of available talent to an organization and the outcomes of current human resources management practices. Clear reporting will help to demonstrate to investors and regulators the actions of the organization towards enhancing human capital, and as such human capital reporting can help to make the case for more sustainable and strategic investment in the workforce. Indicators of interest to external stakeholders include:

- performance-related pay and/or benefits received and the related indicators of performance, including benchmarks of pay;

- investment and outcomes of training related to enhancing employee performance, including leadership development training;

- insights relating to measures of performance over time, including seasonal, geographic and structural differences in measures, to demonstrate variability and reliability.

As well as key performance indicators of human capital performance, the narrative element of annual reports provides an opportunity to describe the way by which human resource strategy is being developed and operationalized to lead and develop workforce performance. Information relating to the impact of performance management systems (eg time-based measures of alignment to espoused values or behaviours to illustrate company culture), or testimonials from senior leadership teams, are common devices in human capital reports to convey both the sentiment and the intention of the organization towards its people. It is for this reason that good-quality human capital reporting includes a mix of quantitative information and insights, and a strong narrative description that both informs and connects with the reader.

Reflective activity

Having read the viewpoint by Edward Houghton consider the following questions:

- How does your organization demonstrate the value of its human capital to external stakeholders?
- How can your organization demonstrate how the workforce is being managed and developed to deliver value to those stakeholders?
- What measures are you currently using, and what data on human capital could you start capturing in the future to demonstrate value?

Evaluation in practice

Back in 2011 Jobcentre Plus introduced a new performance management framework (PMF) to replace the previous targets structure. They conducted an evaluation of the process to assess how well the PMF met its objectives as a more streamlined approach to managing and monitoring performance in Jobcentre Plus. The evaluation considered the following areas:

- Communication – the methods and impact of the communication process relating to the implementation of the PMF.

- Awareness and understanding – the degree to which the purpose of the PMF was understood.

- Managing performance – this evaluated the PMF at operation level. For example, considering the consistency in practices in different parts of the organization.

- Motivation and behaviour – this considered the impact of the PMF on employee motivation and behaviour.

- Governance and transparency – openness and fairness.

- Value for money, and productivity – consideration relating to impact on performance versus investment made.

Adapted from Nunn and Devins (2012) *Process Evaluation of the Jobcentre Plus Performance Management Framework*

You can access the full report on this evaluation process and the outcomes by following the link to the Department for Work and Pensions website (**https://www.gov.uk/government/publications/process-evaluation-of-the-jobcentre-plus-performance-management-framework-rr801**). It highlights the range of considerations that can be taken into account when evaluating a performance management process. Think about whether these evaluation criteria would have relevance in your organization in evaluating the impact of performance management. Which of the tools/methods of evaluation we have explored would most effectively capture the data you require?

Conclusion

Performance management encompasses a wide area of people practice and only so much can be covered in one small book. What I have aimed to do is give you a practically focused overview of performance management and present you with some of the most recent developments and debates in this critical business area. How you use this book moving forward will depend on your own circumstances and the particular context of your organization.

I hope this book provides practical guidance and support to those involved in performance management, be they an HR manager tasked with reviewing and improving an existing performance management process or putting in a performance management infrastructure where nothing has existed before. Maybe you are a line manager taking on direct reports for the first time, seeking guidance on setting objectives, providing feedback and getting the best out of a team. Whatever has drawn you to this book, I hope it has provided some practical guidance that you can take back into action steps in your workplace and maybe also set you on a journey of further research in what I have always found a fascinating subject.

As I stated at the start of this book, much has changed since the first edition in what has been a fairly short space of time. Where we end up in terms of the annual appraisal, ratings, etc, is yet to be seen, but my key message remains the same.

I firmly believe that performance management is at the heart of organization success and however it manifests itself in your organization, it should be recognized as a priority area of organization practice. A starting point is to identify what good performance looks like and then consider the best levers to ensure your organization and the people working within it have the best possible opportunity to achieve it. Whatever you put in place in terms of performance management in your organization, it is never 'job done'. Processes need to be regularly monitored and evaluated to ensure they are still working to drive the performance the organization seeks and enabling your people to do the best work they can.

If you take away one message from this book it should be that effective performance management doesn't need to be complex. People need to know what is expected and why, they need to know how they are doing and what they need to do moving forward to improve/grow performance. Everyone employed by the organization should understand how important their individual contribution is to that organization's success and should feel valued for that contribution. As I said once to a junior employee in the print room of an advertising agency I was helping through the Investors in People Standard: 'You don't just provide the photocopying and distribute mail... you do a fantastic job helping to make superior advertising!'

REFERENCES

ACAS (2013) [accessed 4 December 2013] Workplace Snippet: Minimising the disruption of short-term absences [Online] http://www.acas.org.uk/index.aspx?articleid=4268

Armstrong, M (2006) *A Handbook of Human Resource Management Practice*, Kogan Page, London

Armstrong, M (2009) *Armstrong's Handbook of Performance Management*, Kogan Page, London

Armstrong, M and Baron, A (2005) *Managing Performance*, CIPD

Aylott, E (2014) *Employment Law*, Kogan Page, London

BIS (2014) [accessed 19 February 2018] Does Worker Well-Being Affect Workplace Performance? https://www.gov.uk/government/publications/worker-wellbeing-and-workplace-performance [Online]

Blanchard, K (2011) *The One Minute Manager*, Harper Collins, London

Boyzatis, R E (1982) *The Competent Manager*, Wiley, New York

Brumbach, G B (1998) The complete guide to performance appraisal, *Personnel Psychology*, **51** (1), pp 265–69

Buckingham, M and Coffman, C (1999) *First, Break All the Rules: What the world's greatest managers do differently*, Simon & Schuster, New York

CIPD (2005) Getting the Right Work-Life Balance, in D Currie, *Introduction to HRM*, CIPD 2006

CIPD (2009) *Performance Management in Action: Current trends and practices*, CIPD Survey

CIPD (2014a) *Managing the Value of Your Talent: A new framework for human capital measurement*, CIPD, London

CIPD (2014b) Developing Managers to *Maintain Sustainable Employee Engagement, Health and Well-being*, CIPD, London

CIPD (2016a) Could Do Better? *Assessing what works in performance management*, CIPD, London

CIPD (2016b) *Reporting Human Capital: Illustrating your company's true value*, CIPD, London

CIPD (2016c) *Absence Management Survey Report*, CIPD, London

CIPD (2017a) *Business Ethics and the Role of HR, Fact Sheet*, CIPD, London

CIPD (2017b) *Performance Management: An introduction, Fact Sheet*, CIPD, London

CIPD (2017c) *Strengths-based Performance Conversations: An organisational field trial*, CIPD, London

CIPD (2017d) *Absence Measurement and Management, Fact Sheet*, CIPD, London

Crane, C (2013) [accessed 23 January 2014] New Universal Performance Standard for Civil Servants [Online] www.theguardian.com/public-leaders-network/2013/feb/28/new-civil-service-competency-framework

Deloitte (2015) *Global Human Capital Trends 2015: Leading in the new world of work*, Deloitte University Press

DTI/CIPD (2005) *High-Performance Work Practices: Linking strategy and skills to performance outcomes*, HMSO, London

Furnham, A (1997) *The Psychology of Behaviour at Work*, Psychology Press, Taylor & Francis, Hove

Gallup (2013) [accessed 12 February 2018] *State of the Global Workplace Survey, Gallup* http://www.gallup.com/services/178517/state-global-workplace.aspx [Online]

Goleman, D (1998) *Working with Emotional Intelligence*, Bloomsbury Publishing, London

Goleman, D (2000) Leadership that gets results, *Harvard Business Review*, 78 (2), pp 78–90

Guest, D and Conway, N (1997) *Employee Motivation and the Psychological Contract*, IPD Research Report

Handy, C (2002) *The Age of Unreason*, Random House, London

Harrison, R (2009) *Learning and Development*, CIPD

Herzberg, F (1968) One more time: how do you motivate your employees?, *Harvard Business Review*, Jan–Feb, pp 109–20

Hutchinson, S and Purcell, J (2003) *Bringing Policies to Life: The vital role of front line managers in people management*, CIPD

Institute of Personnel Management (IPM) (1992) *Performance Management in the UK: An analysis of the issues*, London, IPM

Investors in People (IIP) [accessed 14 October 2013] [Online] www.investorsinpeople.co.uk

IRS (2003) Trends in performance management, *Employment Review*, 1 August, pp 12–19

Kaplan, R S and Norton, D P (1996) *The Balanced Scorecard*, Harvard Business School Press, Boston, MA

Kolb, D A (1985) *Experiential Learning: Experience as the source of learning and development*, Prentice Hall, London

Leary-Joyce, J (2004) *Becoming an Employer of Choice*, CIPD

Lewin, K (1947) Frontiers in group dynamics, *Human Relations*, 1 (1), pp 5–41

Locke, E A (1968) Toward a theory of task motivation and incentives, *Organizational Behavior and Human Performance*, 3, pp 137–89

Maitland, A and Thomson, P (2011) *Future Work: How organisations can adapt and thrive in the new way of work*, Palgrave Macmillan, Basingstoke

Marchington, M and Wilkinson, A (2012) *Human Resource Management at Work*, CIPD

Nunn, A and Devins, D (2012) [accessed 29 December 2013] Process Evaluation of the Jobcentre Plus Performance Management Framework [Online] https//www.gov.uk/government/uploads/system/uploads/attachment_data/file/193470/801summ.pdf

Pink, D (2011) *Drive: The surprising truth about what motivates us*, Canongate, London

Porter, M E (1985) *Competitive Advantage: Creating and sustaining performance*, Free Press, New York

Purcell, J, Kinnie, N, Hutchinson, S, Rayton, B and Swart, J (2003) *Understanding the People and Performance Link: Unlocking the black box*, CIPD

PWC (2017) [accessed 23 October 2017] *Workforce of The Future: The competing forces shaping 2030* https://www.pwc.com/gx/en/services/people-organisation/workforce-of-the-future/workforce-of-the-future-the-competing-forces-shaping-2030-pwc.pdf [Online]

Rayton B, Dodge T, D'Analeze, G (2012) *Engage for Success: The evidence* [Online] http://engageforsuccess.org/wp-content/uploads/2015/09/The-Evidence.pdf

Rousseau, D (1998) The 'problem' of the psychological contract considered, *Journal of Organizational Behaviour*, **19** (special edn), pp 665–71

Ruble, T and Thomas, K (1976) Two-dimensional model of conflict behaviour, in G Watson and K Gallagher (2005) *Managing for Results*, CIPD, London

Sisson, K and Storey, J (2000) *The Realities of Human Resource Management*, Open University Press, Milton Keynes

Stiles, P, Gratton, L, Truss, C, Hope-Hailey, V and McGovern, P (1997) Performance management and the psychological contract, *Human Resource Management Journal*, **7** (1), pp 56–57

Storey, J (1992) *Developments in the Management of Human Resources*, Blackwell, Oxford

Storey, J (1995) *Human Resource Management: A critical text*, Routledge, London

Taylor, S (2008) *People Resourcing*, CIPD

Ulrich, D (1998) A new mandate for human resources, *Harvard Business Review*, **76** (1), Jan–Feb, pp 124–34

Ulrich, D and Brockbank, W (2005) *The Value Proposition*, Harvard Business School Press, Boston

Wilton, N (2011) *An Introduction to HRM*, Sage, London

INDEX

Note: Page numbers in *italics* indicate Figures or Tables.

More titles in this series

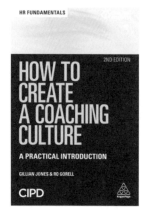

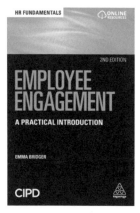

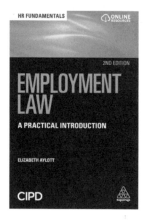

Performance Management is one of the titles in
Kogan Page's HR Fundamentals series,
which is endorsed by the CIPD.

Succint, practical guides for students
and people starting a career in HR.

Find out more at
www.koganpage.com/HRFundamentals

 @KPCoachHR

HR FUNDAMENTALS